Paris and Glen Morris Ontario in Photos, Saving Our History One Photo at a Time

Photography
by Barbara Raué
2013

Series Name:
Cruising Ontario

Book 25: Paris and Glen Morris

Cover photo: Railway bridge over the Grand River

Series Name: Cruising Ontario

Book 1: London
Book 2: Dundas
Book 3: Hamilton
Book 4: Oakville
Book 5: Chesley
Book 6: Stoney Creek
Book 7: Waterdown
Book 8: Owen Sound
Book 9: Mount Forest
Book 10: Dundalk
Book 11: Burford and Area
Book 12: Waterford and Area
Book 13: Drumbo and Area
Book 14: Sheffield and Area
Book 15: Tavistock and Area
Book 16: Ancaster and Mount Hope
Book 17: Innerkip
Book 18: Brantford
Book 19: Burlington
Book 20: Guelph and Area
Book 21: Ayr
Book 22: Erin
Book 23: Goderich
Book 24: Lucknow and Area
Book 25: Paris and Glen Morris
Book 26: Toronto
Book 27: Beaver Valley
Book 28: Collingwood
Book 29: Peterborough
Book 30: Orangeville Beginnings Part 1
Book 31: Orangeville Part 2 and Area
Book 32: Port Elgin

Other Books by Barbara Raue

Coins of Gold

Arrows, Indians and Love

The Life and Times of Barbara
Volume 1: Inventions That Have Enhanced My Life
Volume 2: Entertainment That I Have Enjoyed
Volume 3: East Coast Trips
Volume 4: Olympics Have Always Intrigued Me
Volume 5: Wonders of the World
Volume 6: Caribbean Cruises We Have Enjoyed
Volume 7: Animals
Volume 8: Storms and Other Major Disasters in My Lifetime
Volume 9: Wars, Terrorist Attacks and Major Disasters

The Cromwell Family Book

Visit Barbara's website to view all of her books
http://barbararaue.ericraue.com

Paris

Paris, Ontario is located on the Grand River. It was first settled by Hiram Capron a native of Vermont who, in 1822, emigrated to Norfolk County where he helped to establish one of Upper Canada's earliest iron foundries. He settled here at the Forks of the Grand (where the Grand and Nith Rivers meet) in 1829, divided part of his land into town lots, and in 1830 constructed a grist-mill and named the town after the gypsum deposits that were mined nearby. Gypsum is used to make plaster of Paris. The town of Paris is often referred to as the "cobblestone capital of Canada" because of the many cobblestone buildings that are still standing. Cobblestone architecture refers to the use of cobblestones embedded in mortar to erect walls of houses and commercial buildings.

Glen Morris

Glen Morris is located on East River Road, Brant County Road #14. The German Woolen Mill was built in 1867 and operated for several years. The Glen Morris General Store is located at 57 Princess Street. Glen Morris is located about 22.4 kilometres northwest of Brantford, about 11 kilometres southwest of Cambridge, and about 11 kilometres northeast of Paris.

Downtown – storefront facades

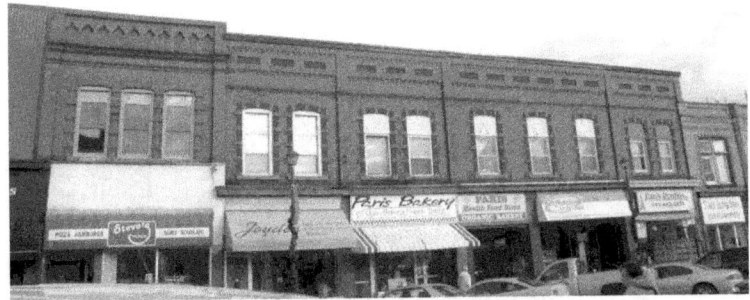

Dentil moulding

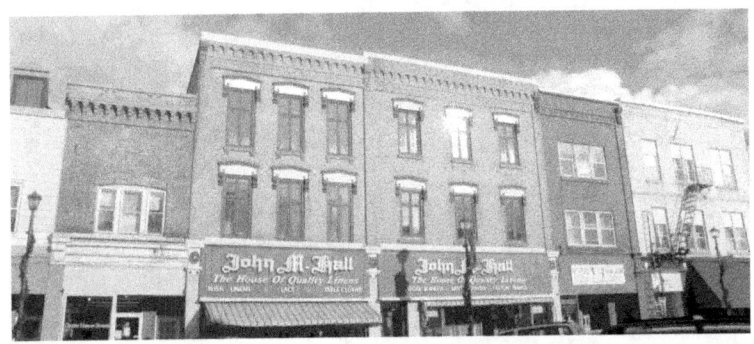

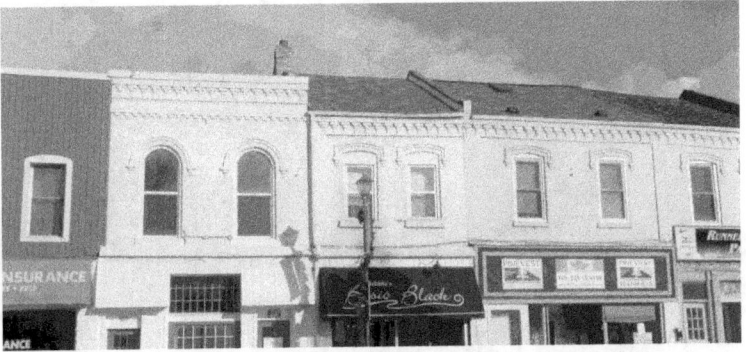

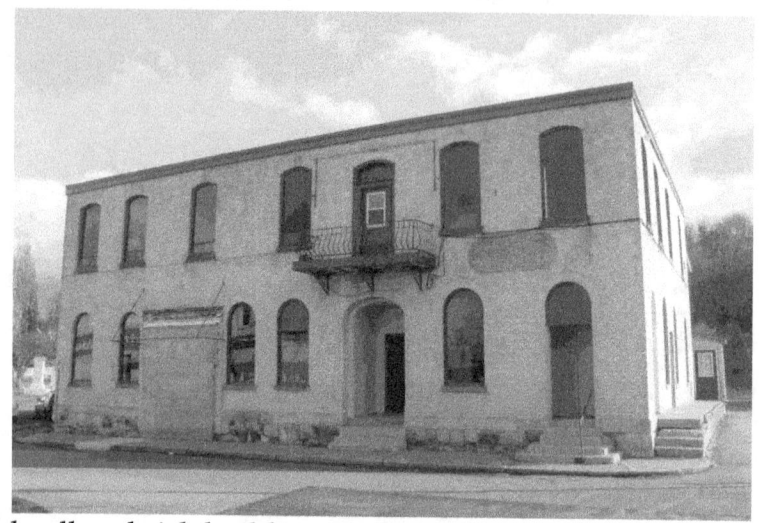

Old yellow brick building, arched windows, iron cresting for second floor balcony

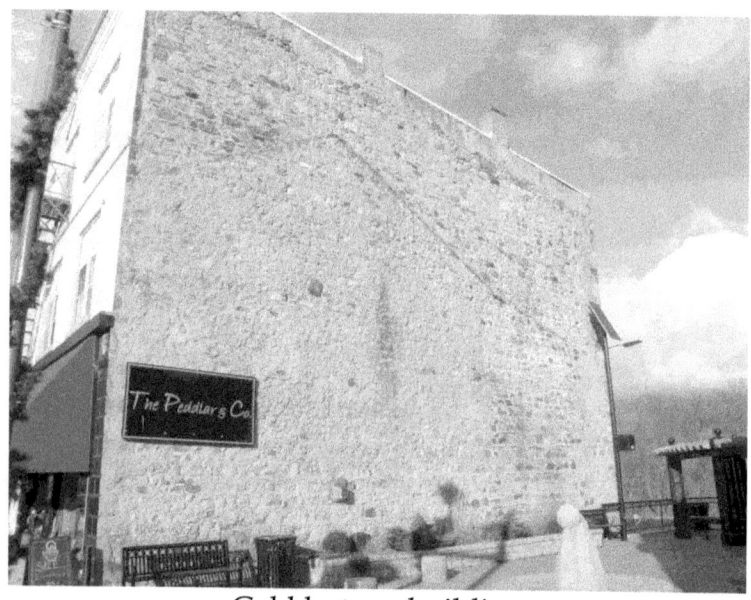

Cobblestone building

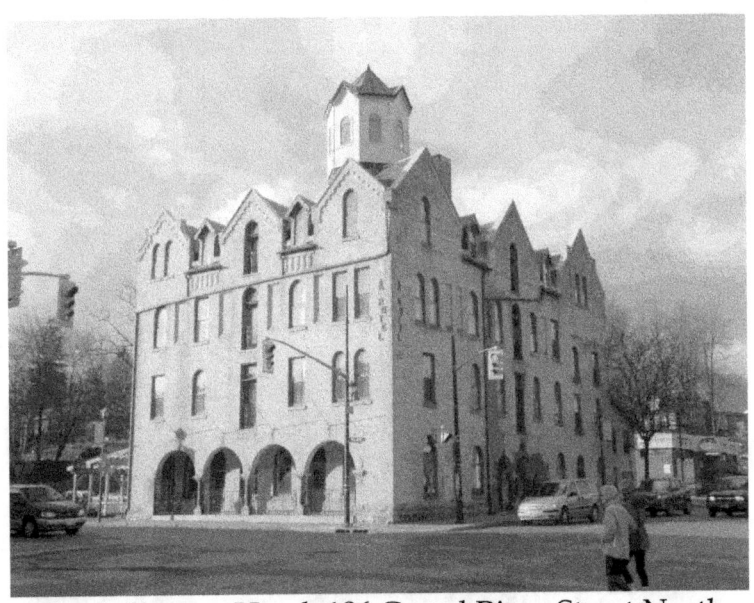

The Arlington Hotel, 106 Grand River Street North
c. 1850s – 4-storey stucco and yellow brick reminiscent of the Chateau style, Romanesque style arcades supported by red-brown marble columns at the street level, octagonal tower, arched and rectangular windows

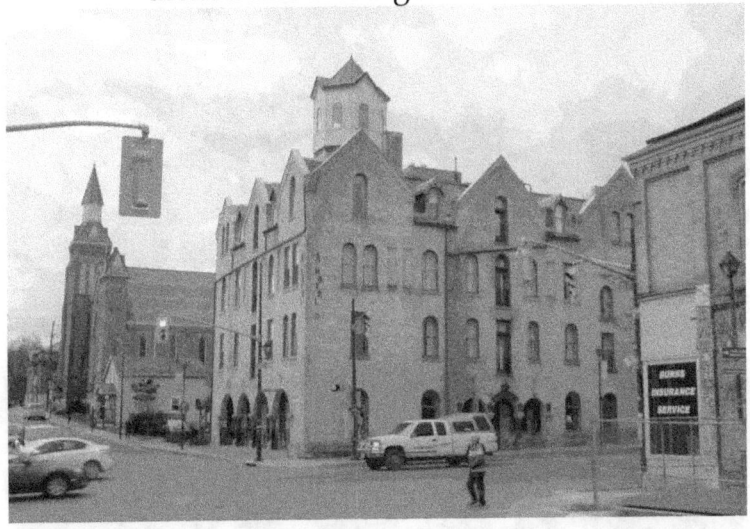

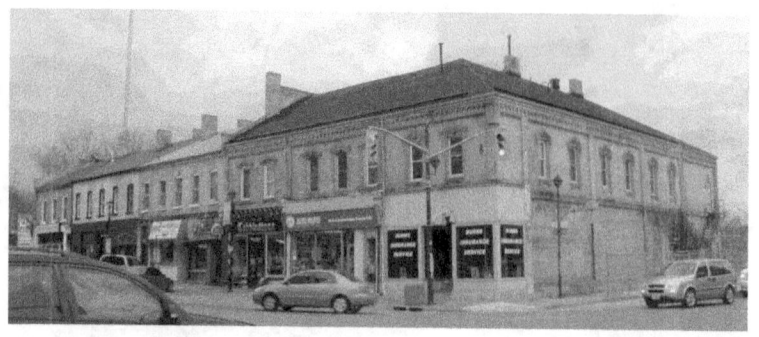

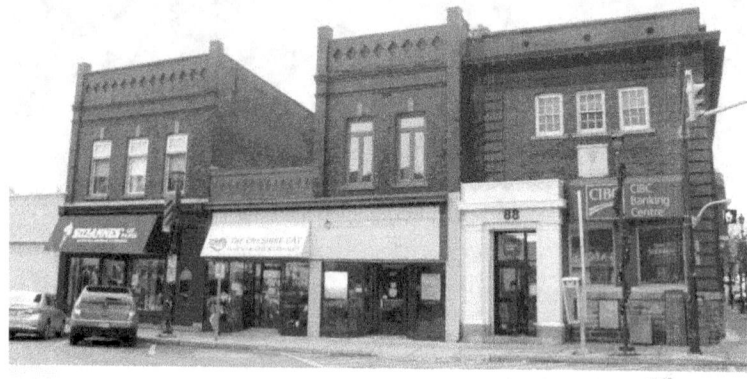

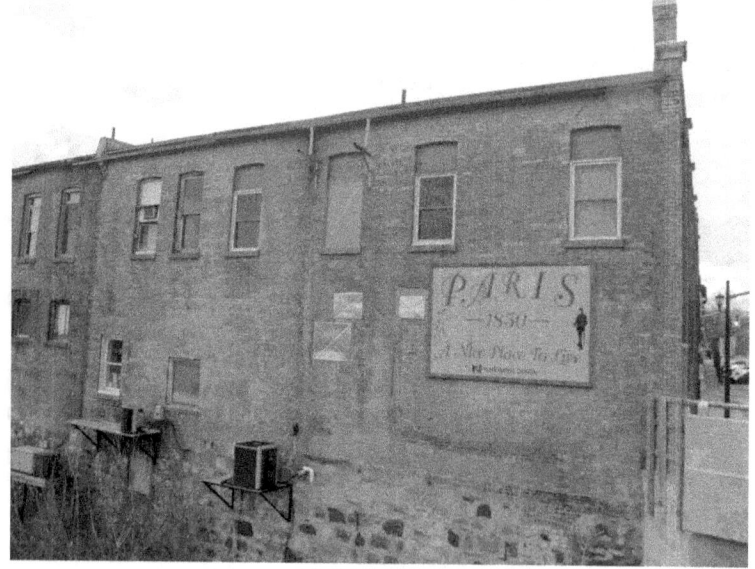

Cobblestone

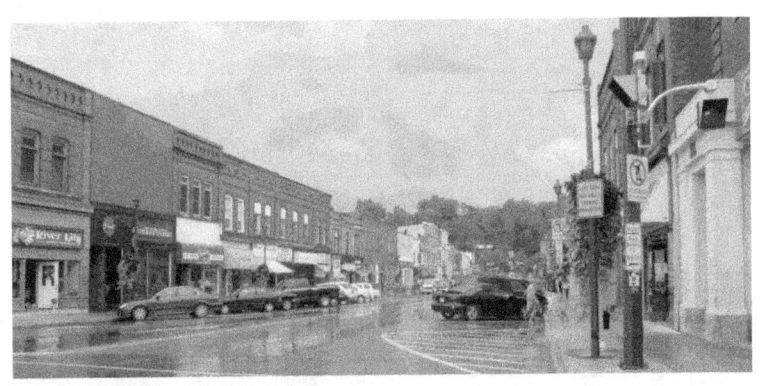

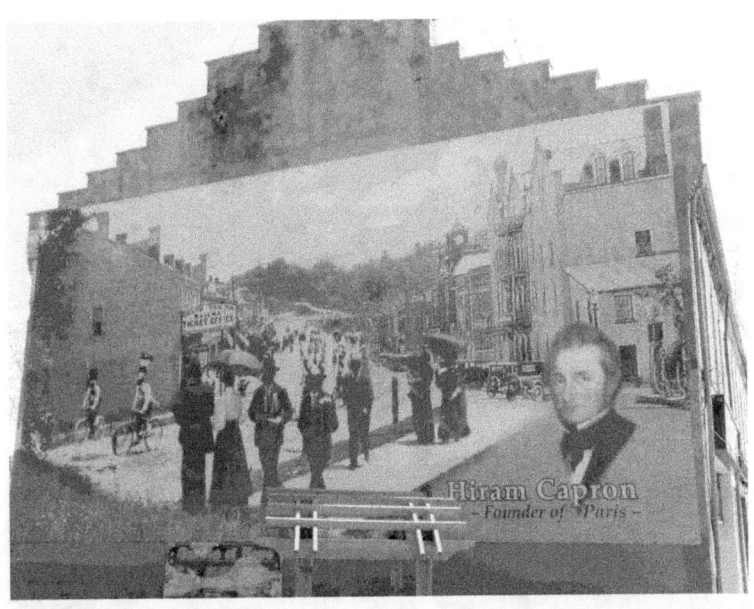

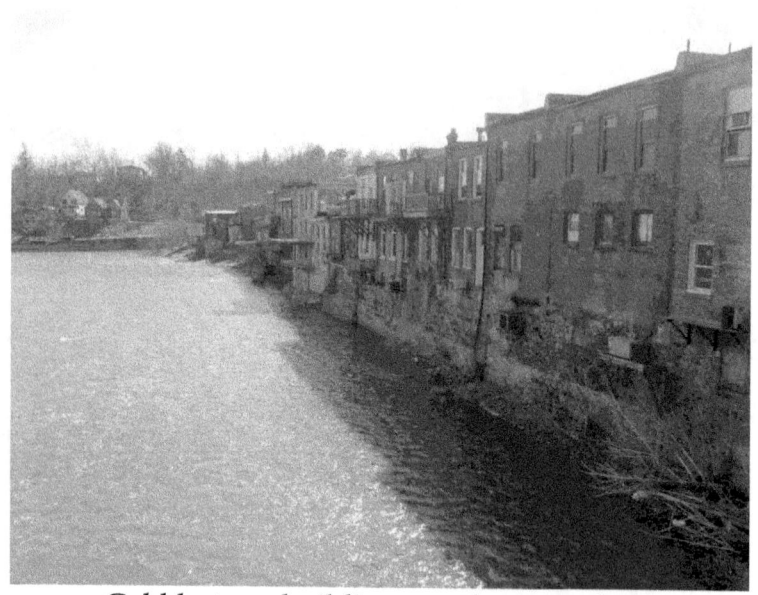
Cobblestone buildings on the waterfront

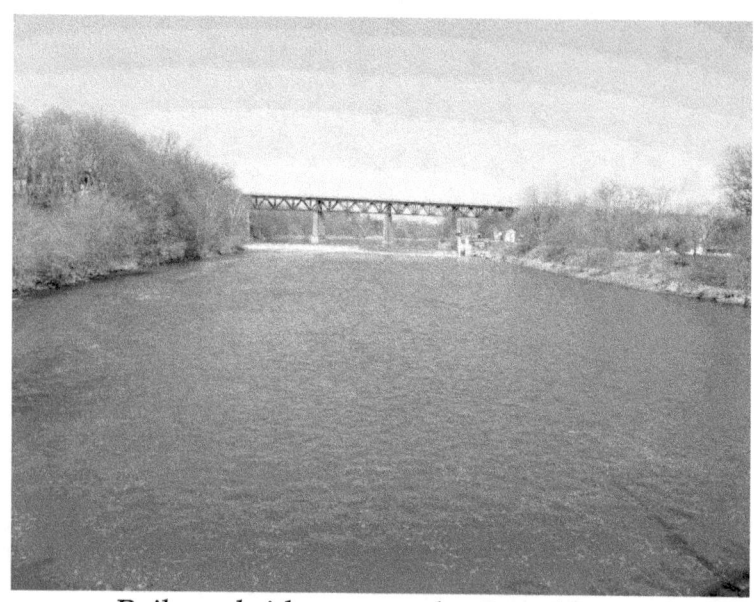
Railway bridge across the Grand River

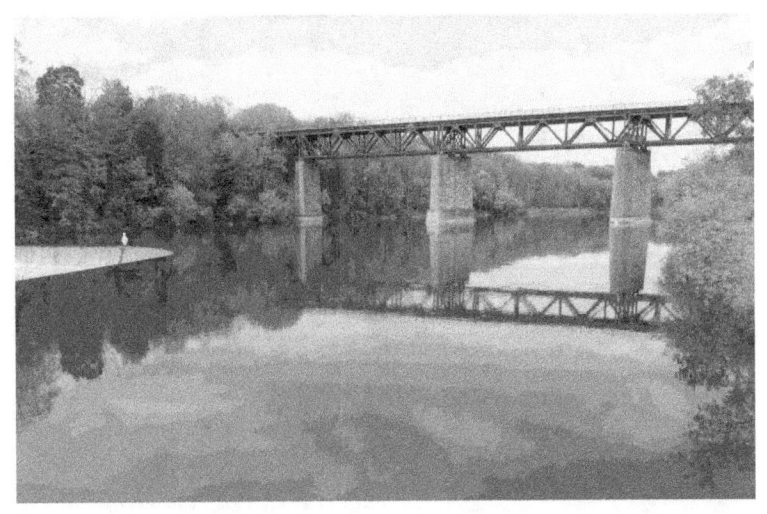

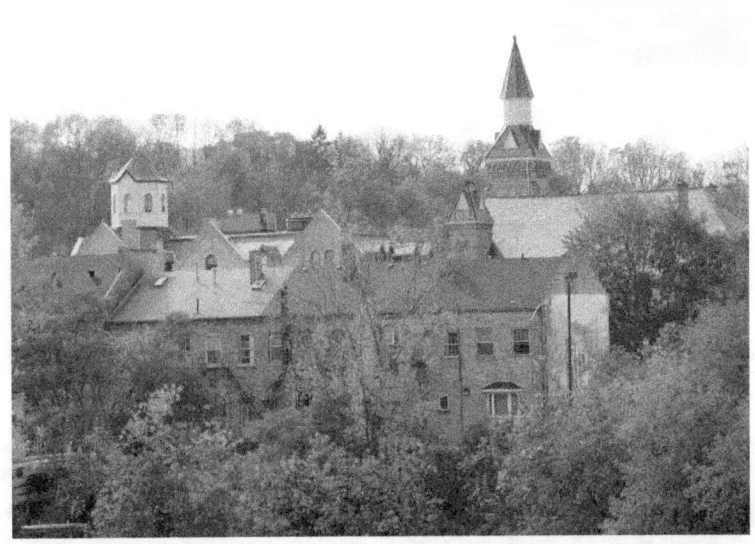

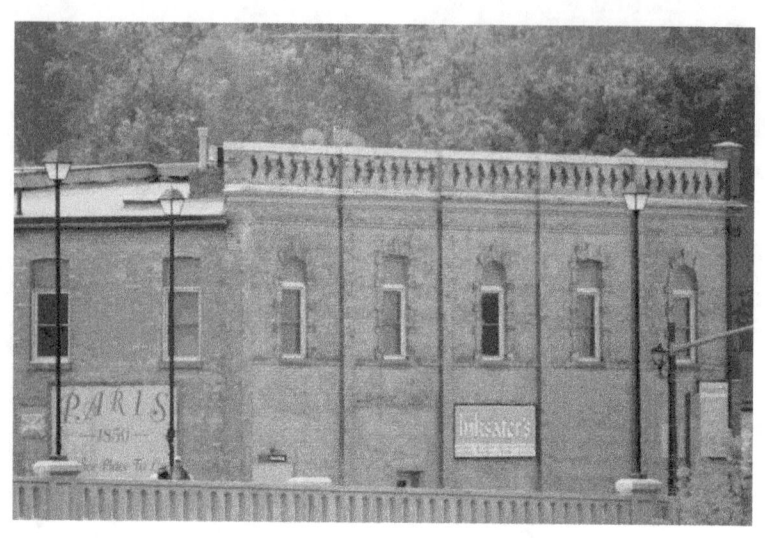

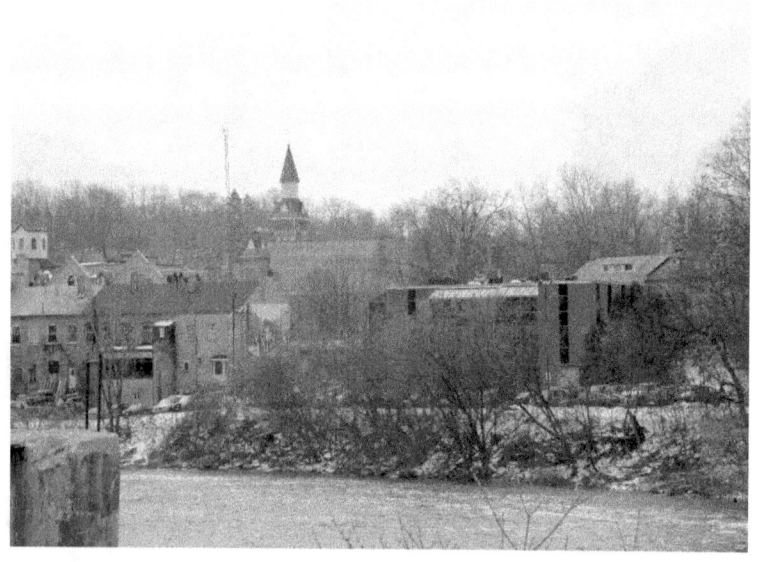

Willow Street

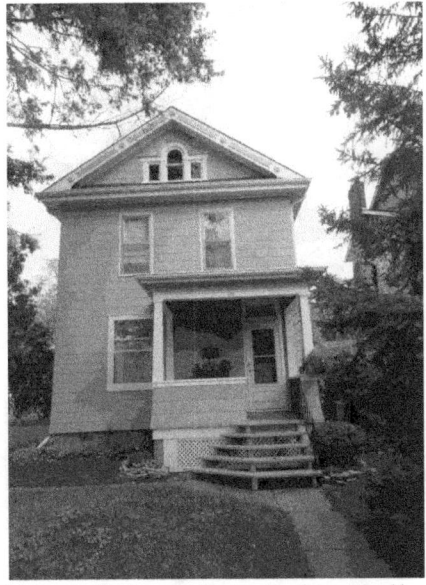

111 Willow Street – Edwardian style – Palladian window

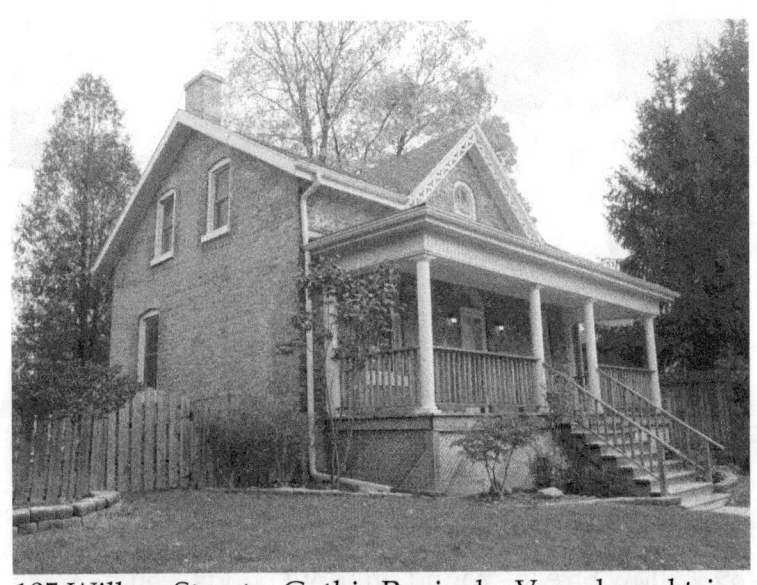

105 Willow Street – Gothic Revival – Vergeboard trim, cobblestone

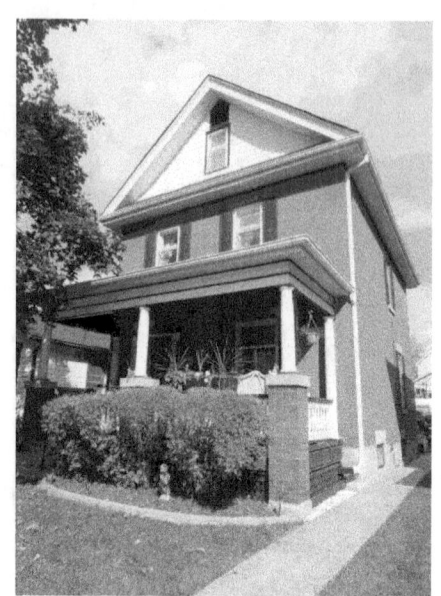

95 Willow Street

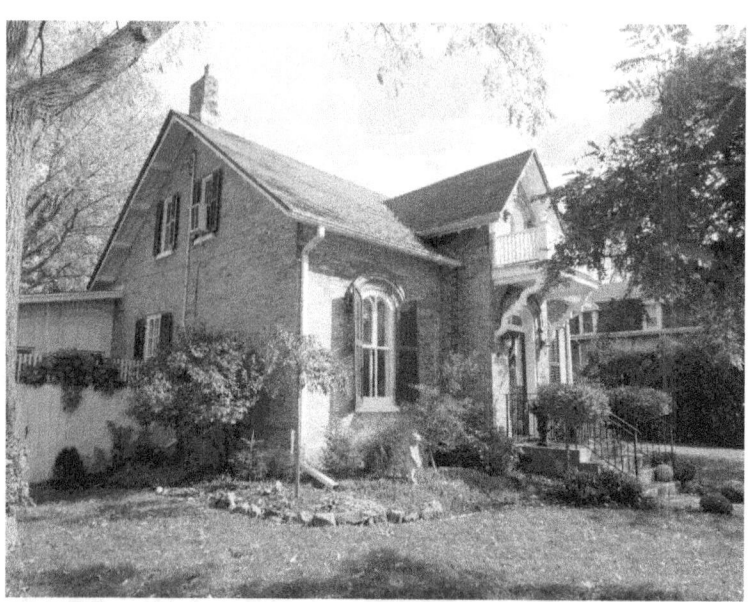

89 Willow Street – round window hoods, yellow brick

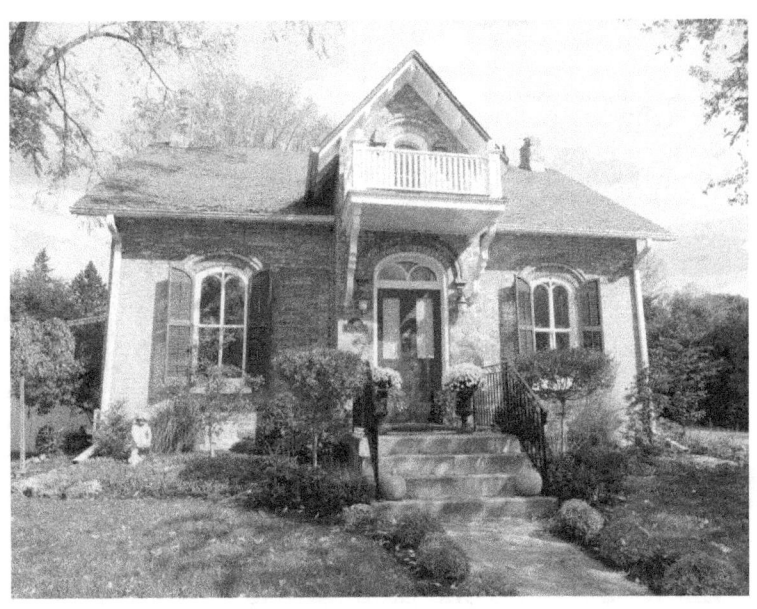

89 Willow Street - Gothic Revival, 1½ storey,

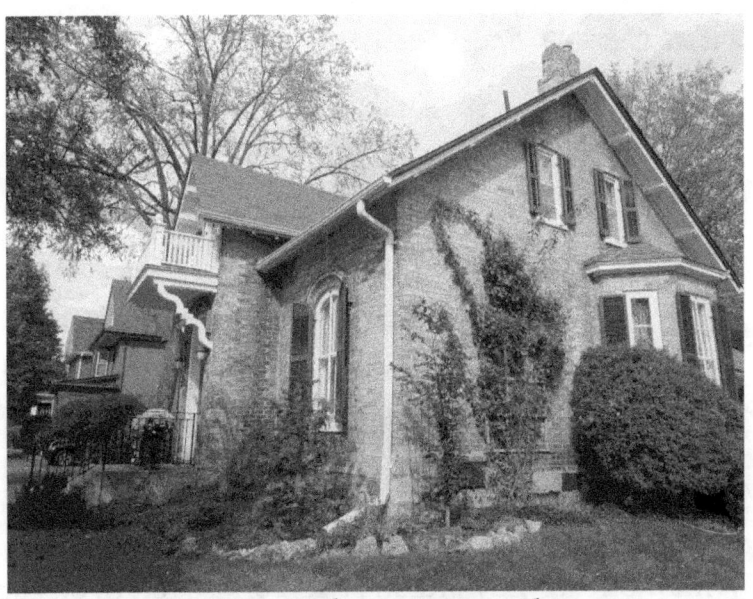

Bay window on one end

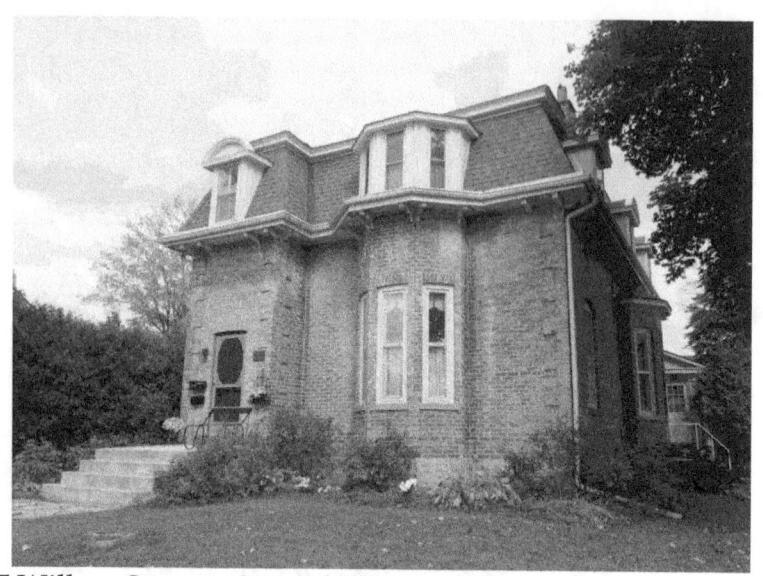

87 Willow Street – Second Empire style – mansard roof, tall windows, elliptical dormers

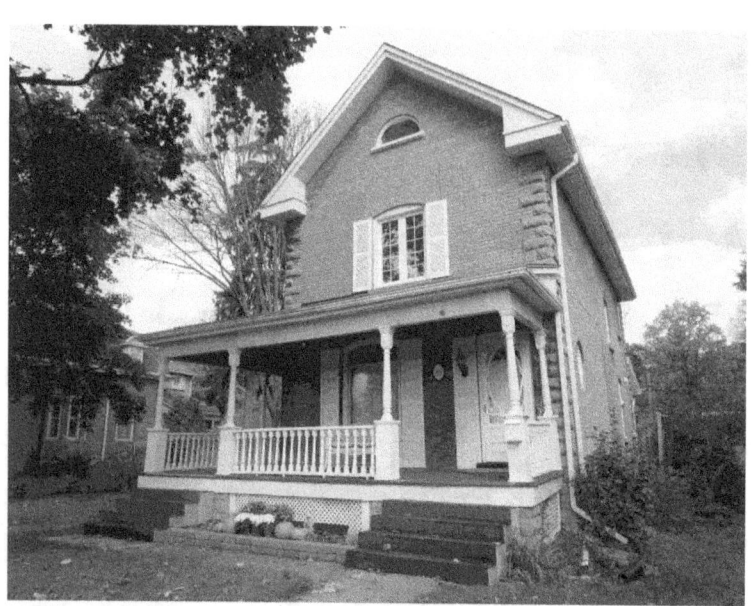

83 Willow Street – Edwardian Style, cornice return on gable, quoining on corners

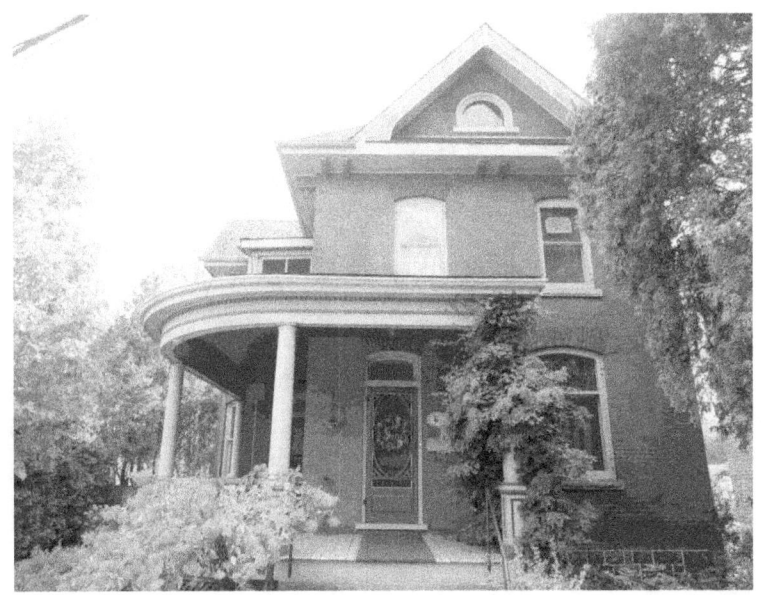

61 Willow Street – Edwardian style – large front porch, smooth red brick surface

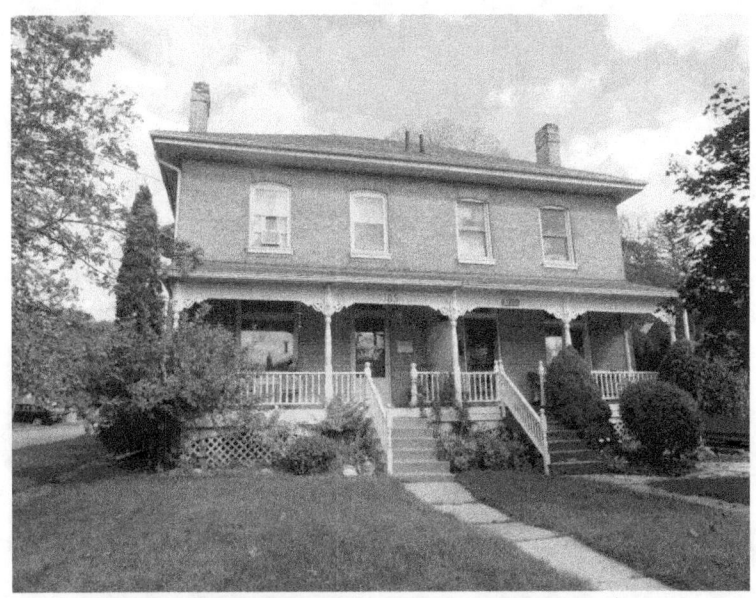

83, 85 William Street – Georgian style

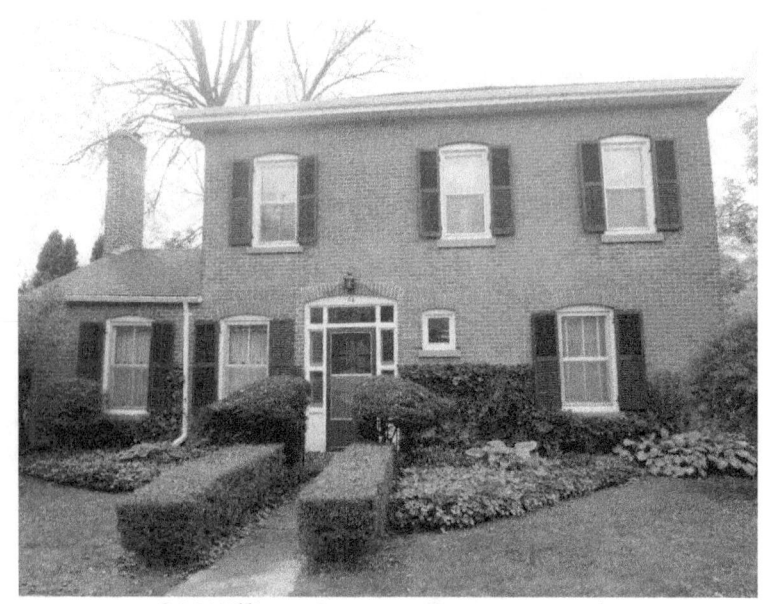

84 William Street – Georgian style

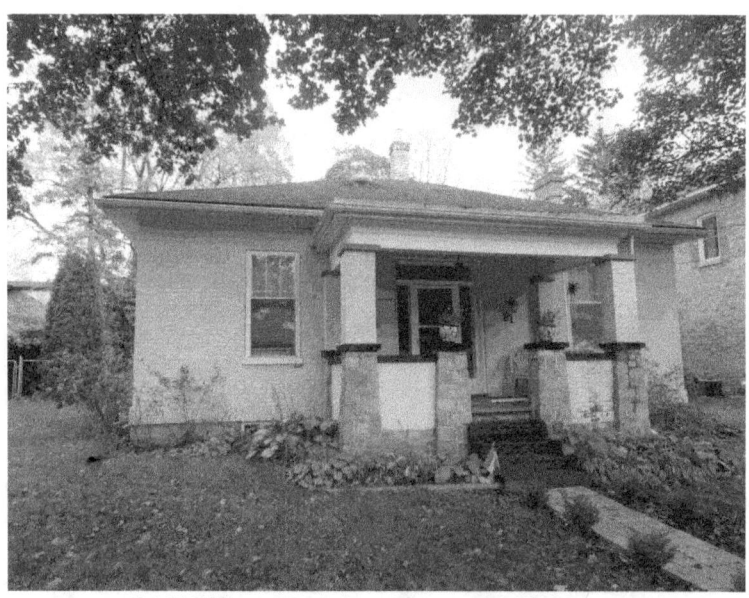

81 William Street – Regency Cottage

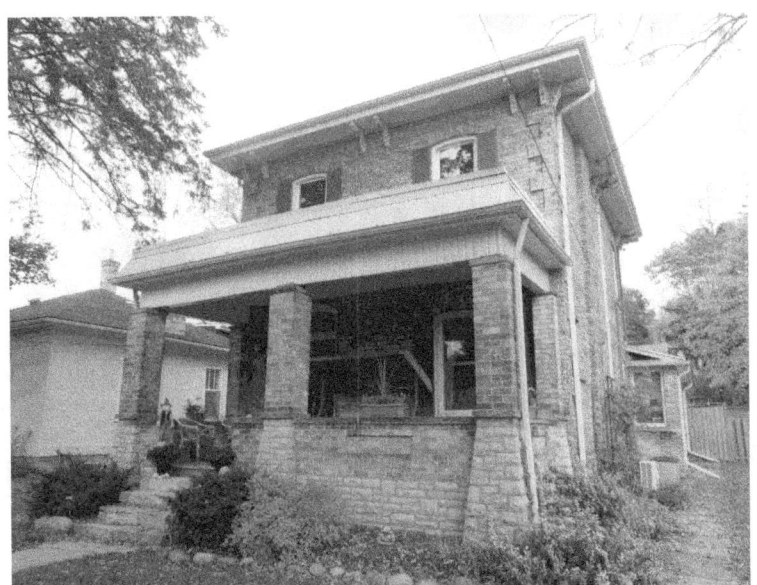

79 William Street – Italianate style – paired cornice brackets,

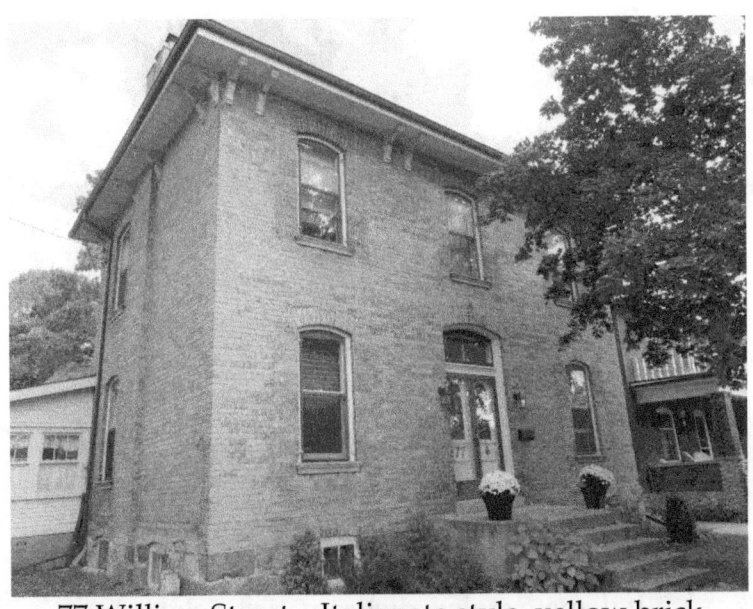

77 William Street – Italianate style, yellow brick

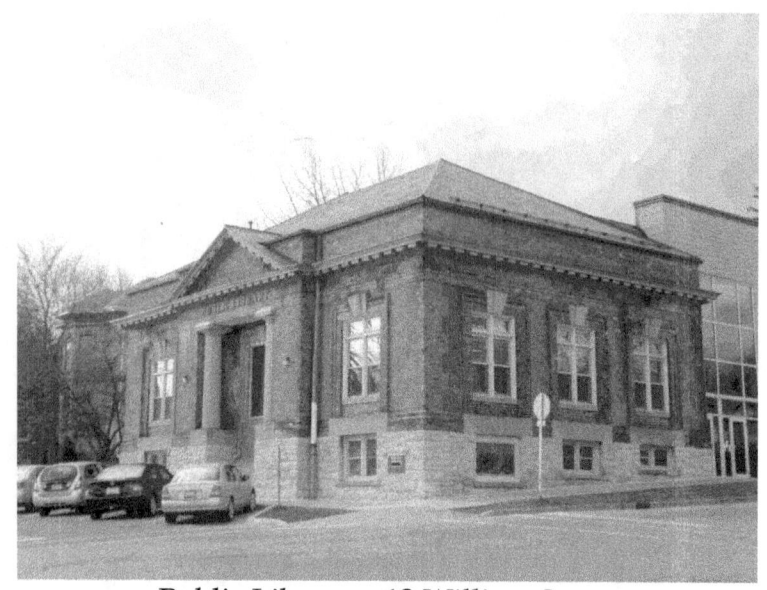

Public Library – 12 William Street

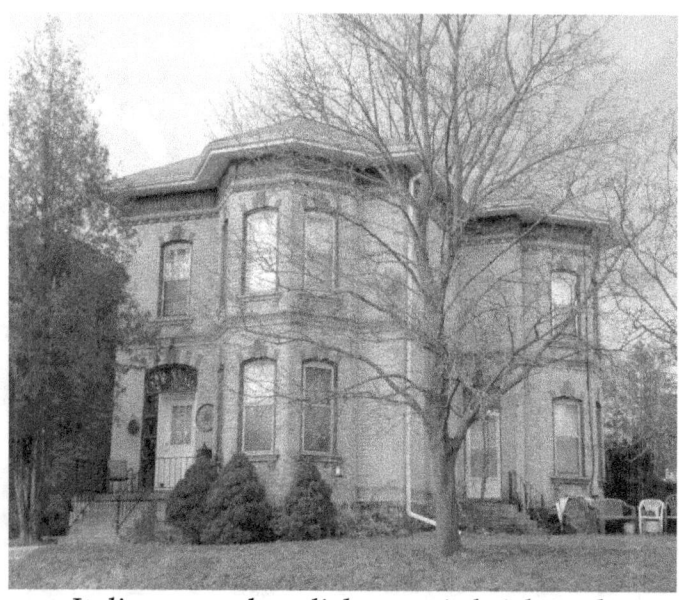

Italianate style – dichromatic brickwork

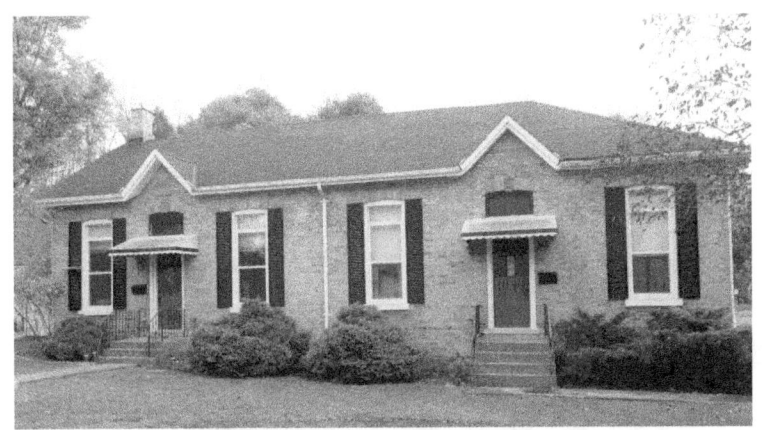

73, 75 William Street – Gothic Revival Cottage

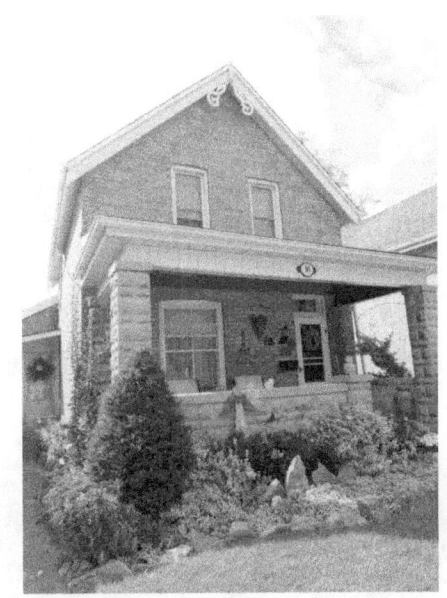

96 William Street – Gothic Revival

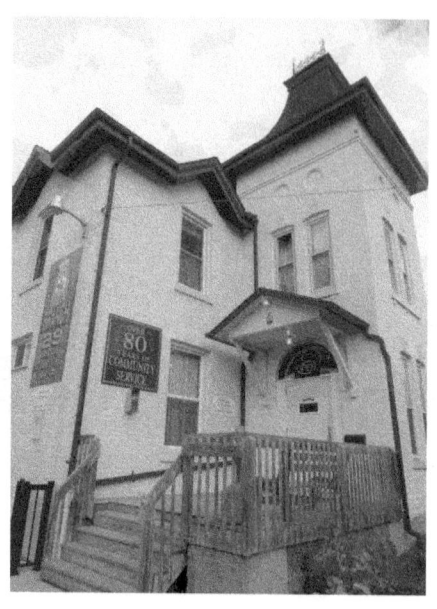

70 William Street – Branch 29 Royal Canadian Legion

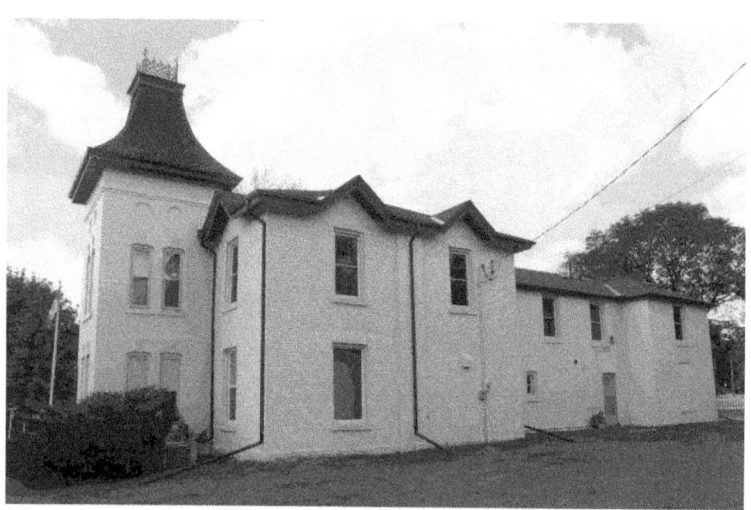

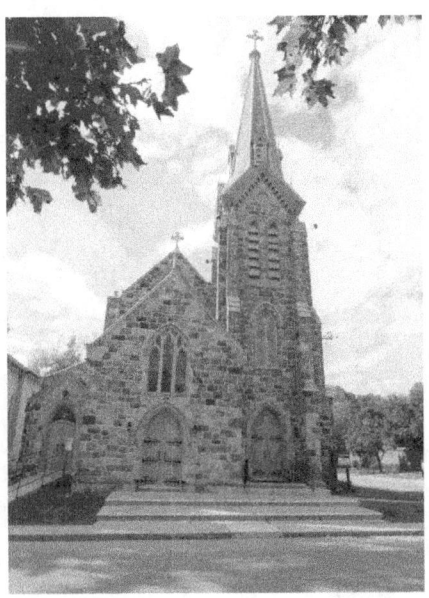

Sacred Heart Church – 17 Washington Street

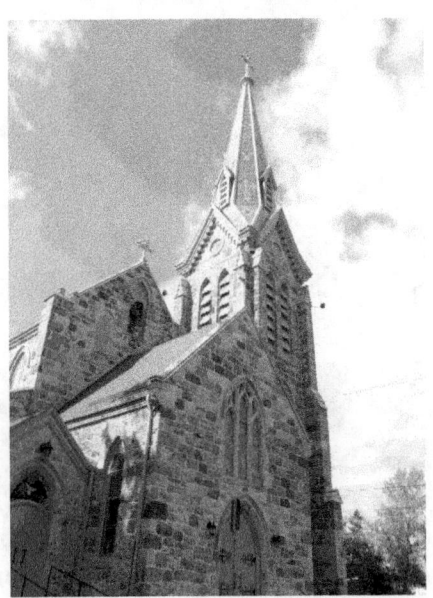

Dichromatic tile work on the spire, cobblestone

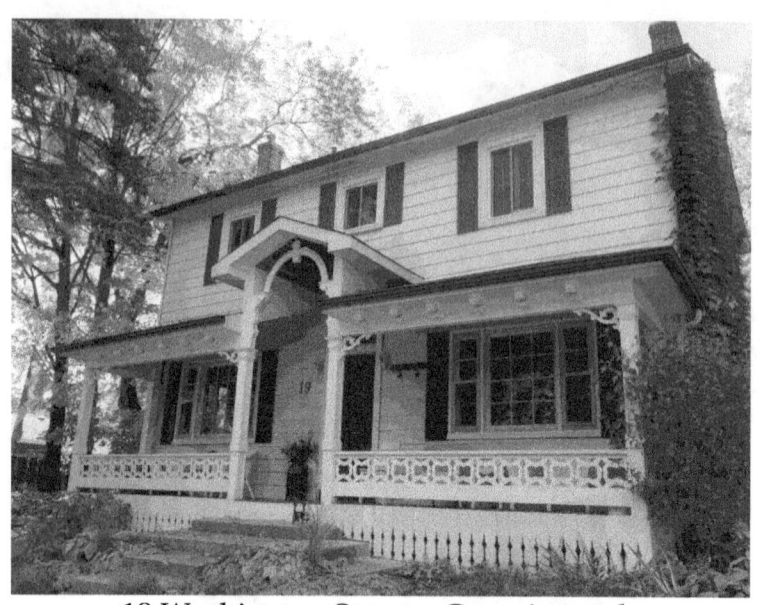

19 Washington Street – Georgian style

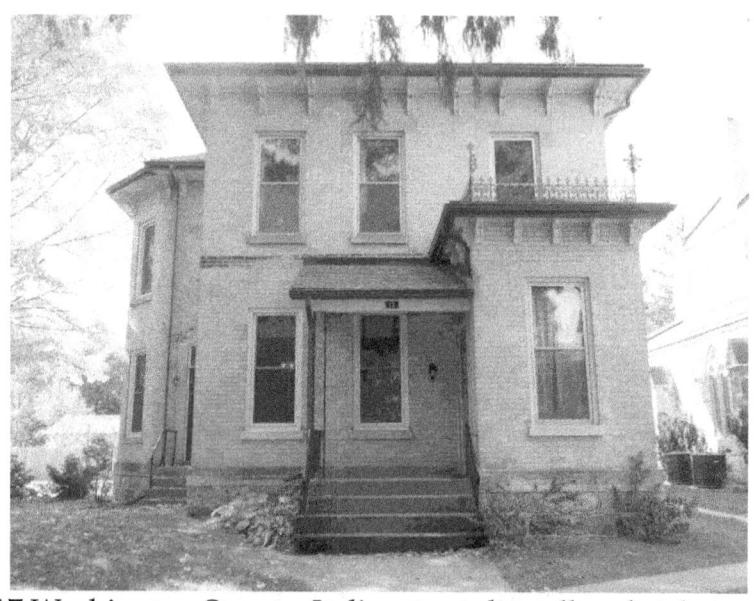

17 Washington Street – Italianate style, yellow brick, iron cresting above square bay window, single cornice brackets

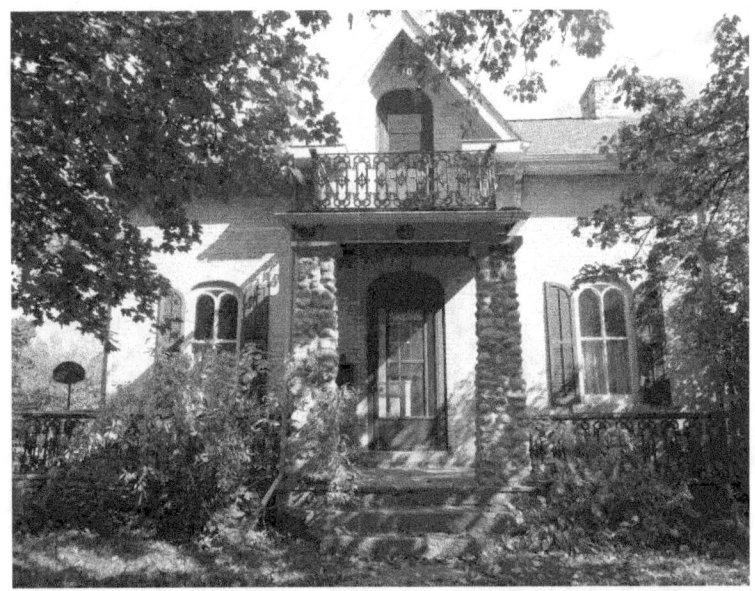

Washington Street – Gothic Revival, yellow brick, iron cresting above door, cornice return on gable, cobblestone pillars

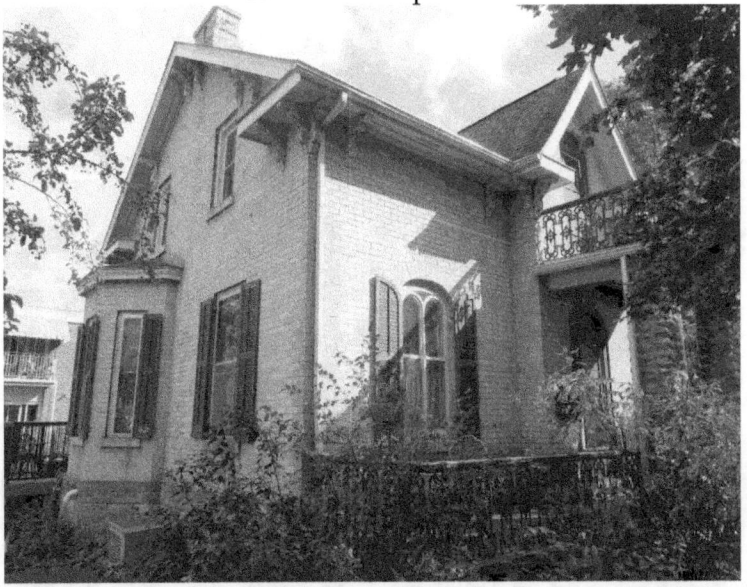

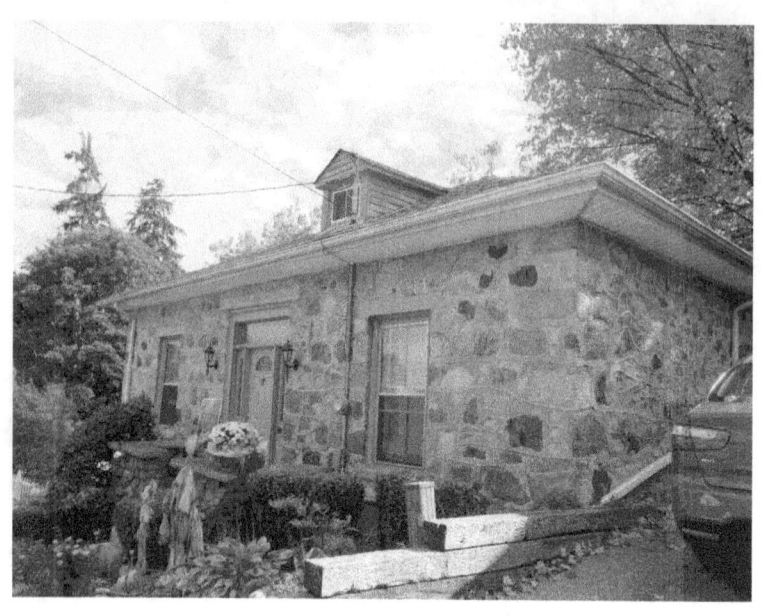

57 Main Street – cobblestone Regency Cottage

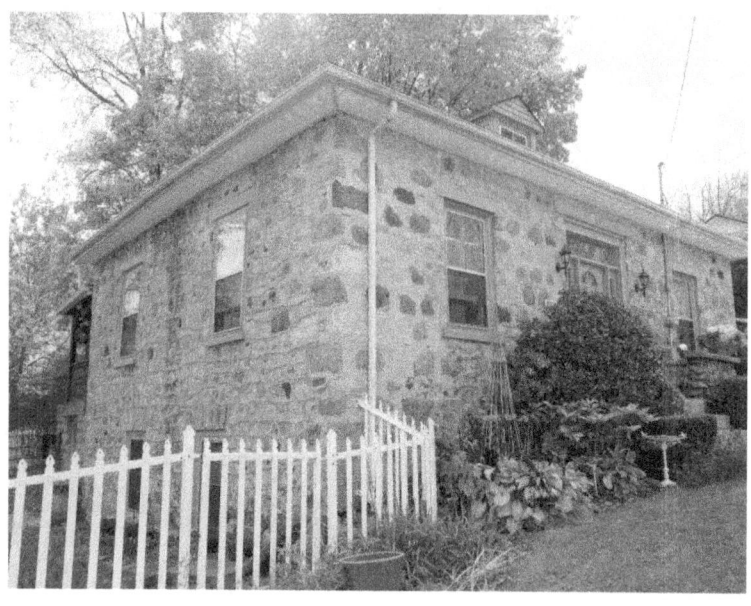

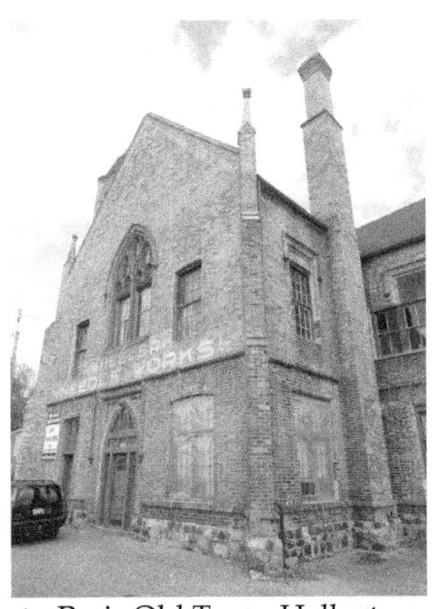

13 Burwell Street - Paris Old Town Hall, at one time it housed Wheeler Needle Works – Gothic Revival style - 1854

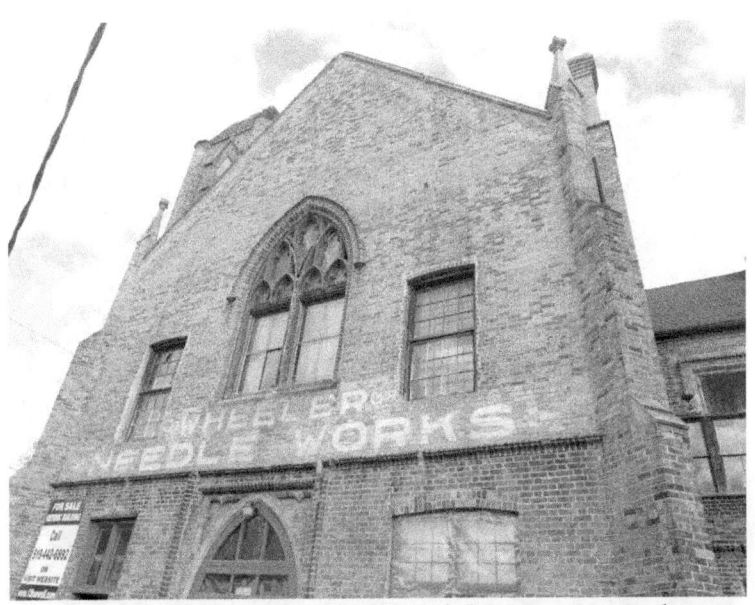

Strongly ecclesiastical style of the centre window

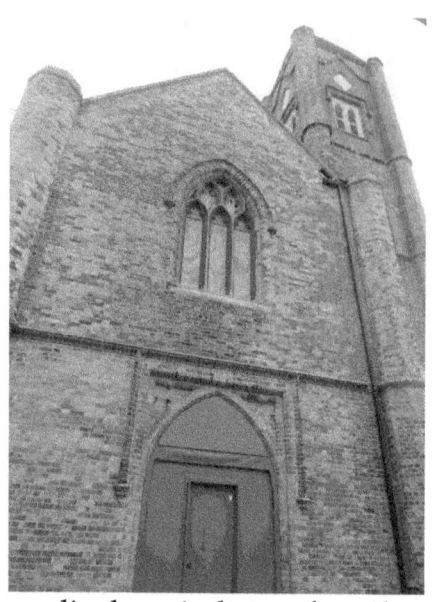

Three-light perpendicular windows of north and south fronts, rectangular moulded frame for the doorway, the octagonal clasping buttresses at the angles of the wings and the tower

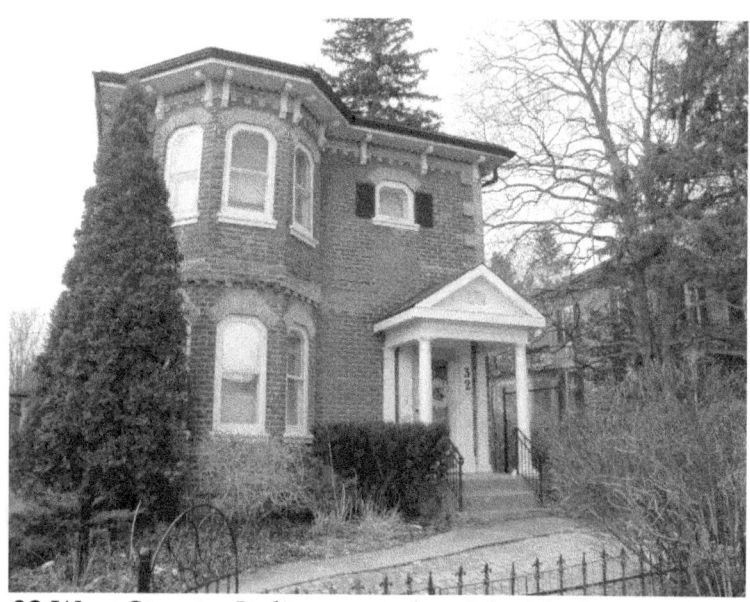

32 West Street – Italianate style with side frontispiece, triangular pediment over doorway with round pillars

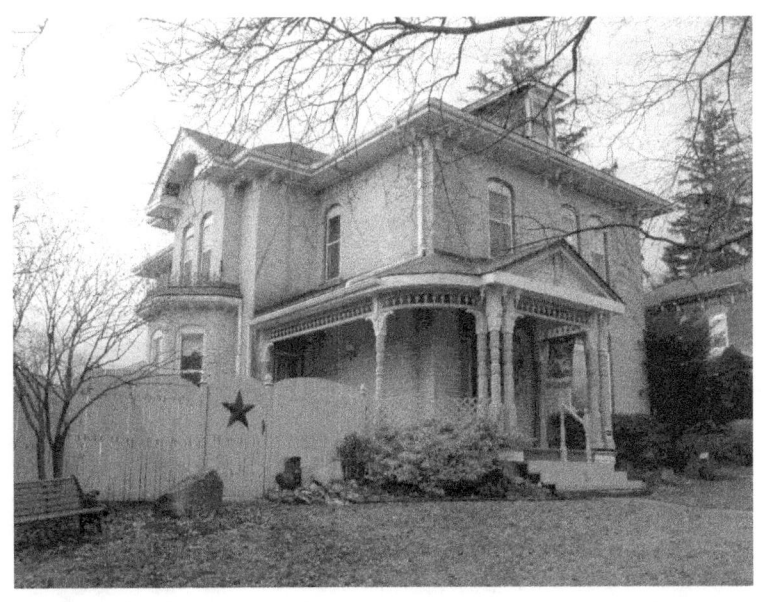

Iron cresting above bay window on the side
28 West Street – Italianate style, paired cornice brackets

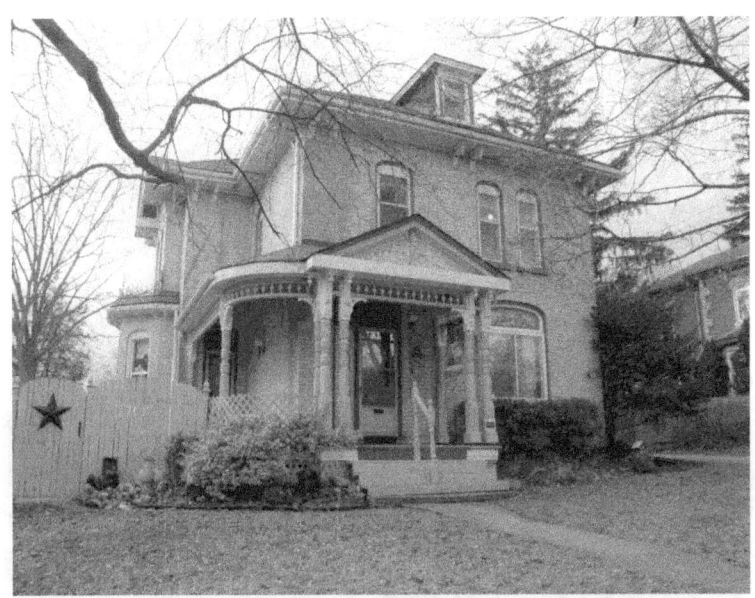

Triangular pediment above doorway

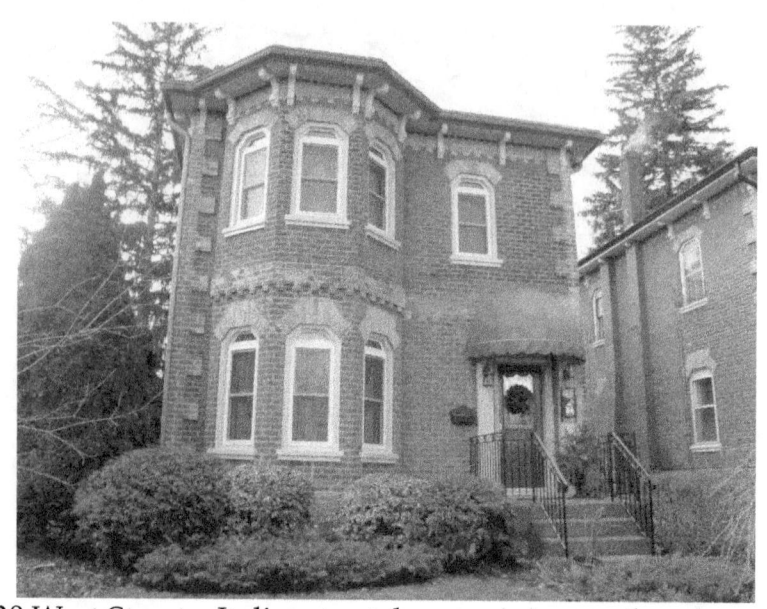

30 West Street – Italianate style – quoining on the corners, paired cornice brackets, dentil brickwork under the cornice, two storey frontispiece raised from the rest of the building with brick ornamentation

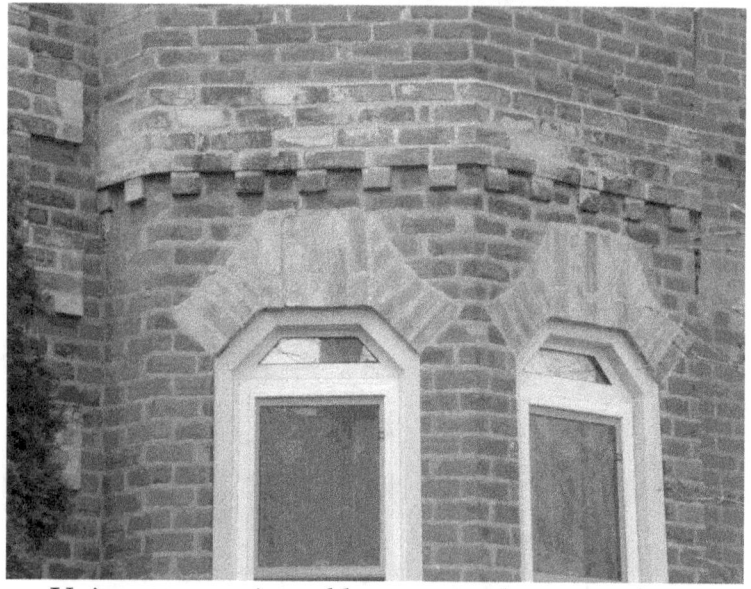

Unique voussoir and keystones above windows

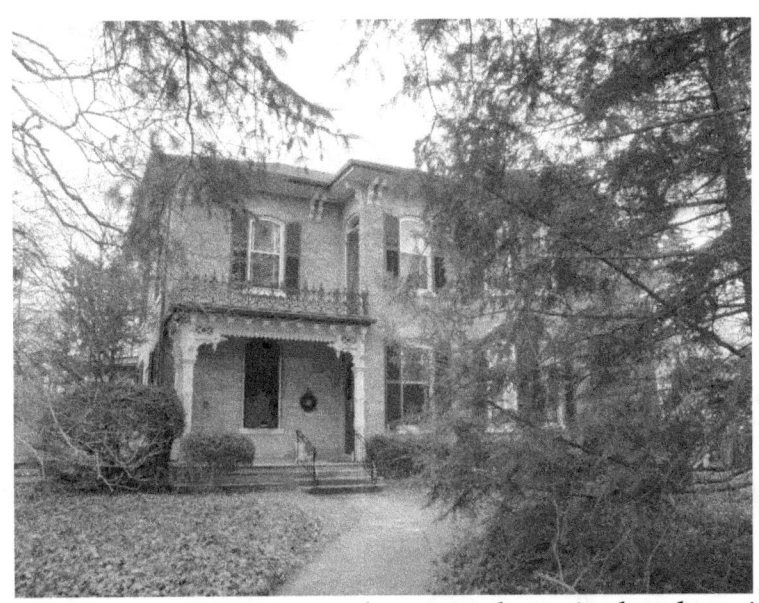

36 West Street – Italianate style – paired cornice brackets, iron cresting around second floor balcony

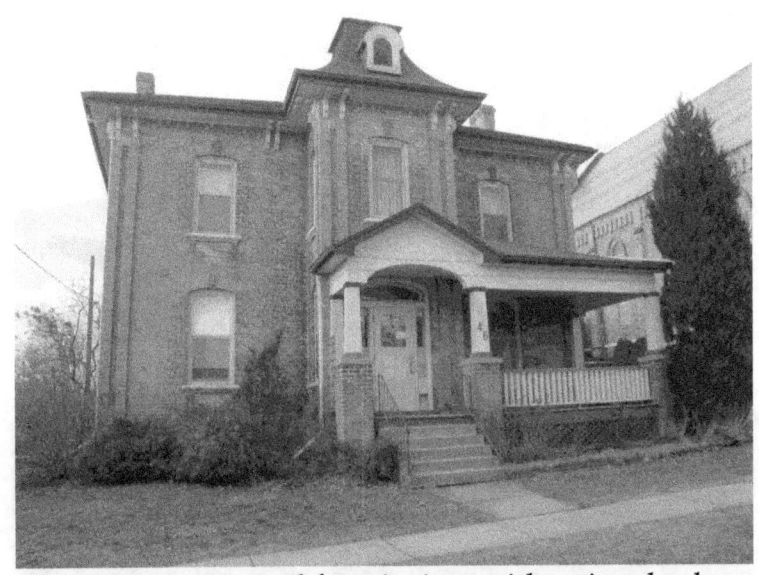

46 West Street – central frontispiece with uniquely shaped ornamental rooftop

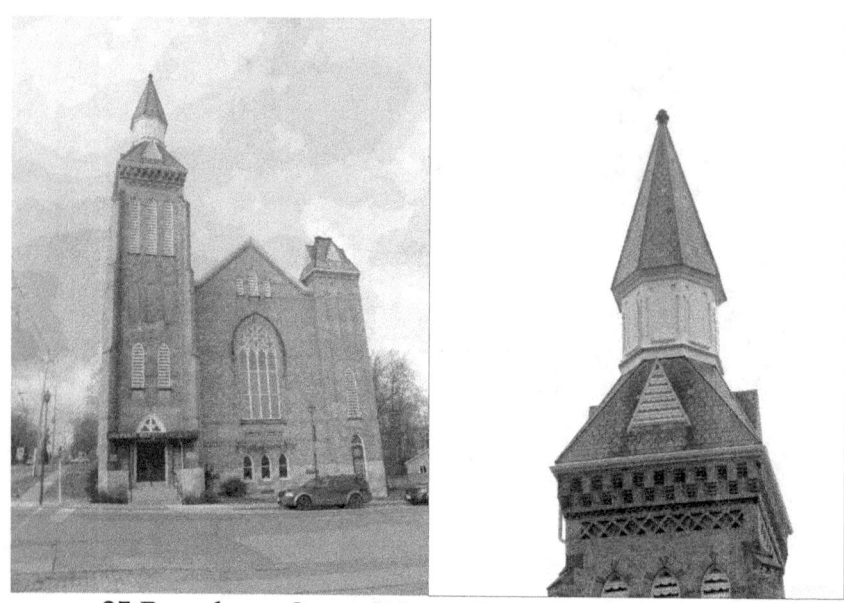

25 Broadway Street West – Paris Baptist Church
Yellow brick with dichromatic banding, and dichromatic tiling on the tower tops

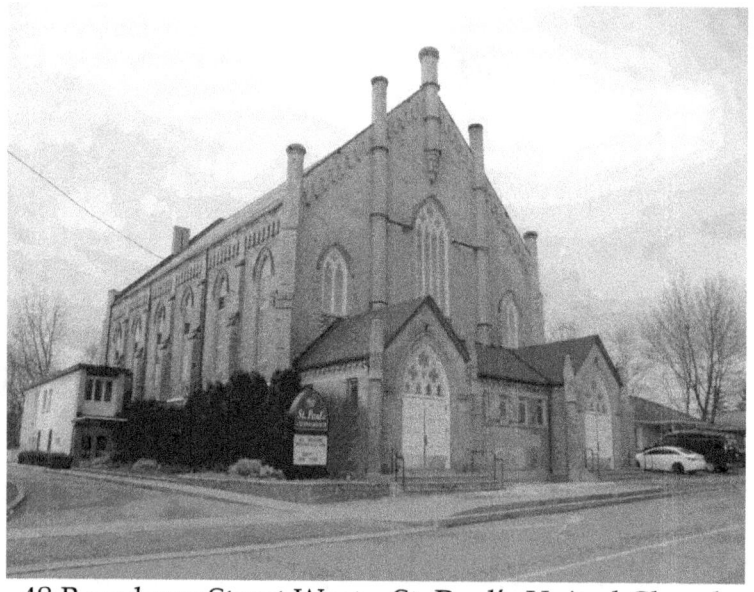

48 Broadway Street West – St. Paul's United Church
Yellow brick, dentil moulding, lancet windows

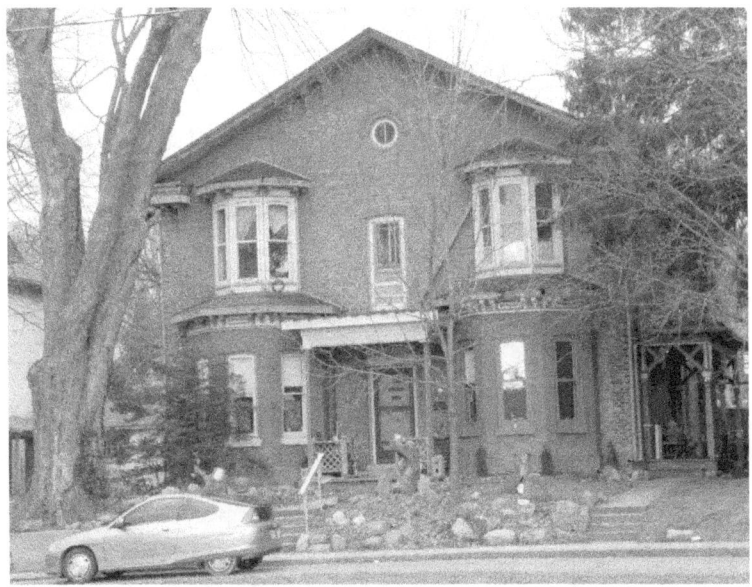

Broadway Street West – Gothic Revival with Italianate features, two storey bay windows

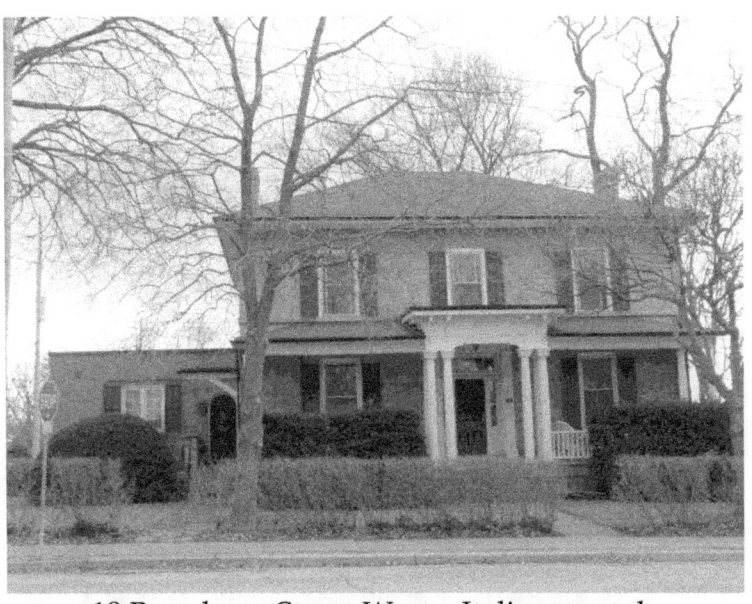

19 Broadway Street West – Italianate style

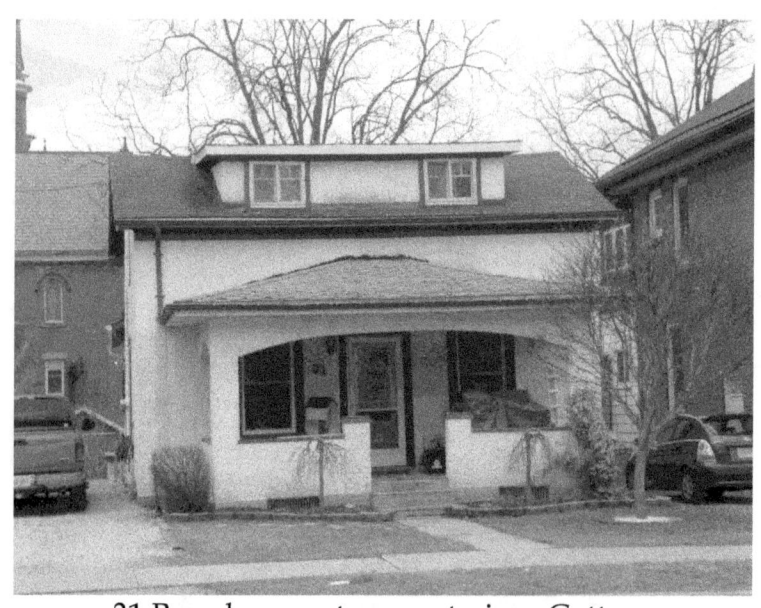

31 Broadway – stucco exterior - Cottage

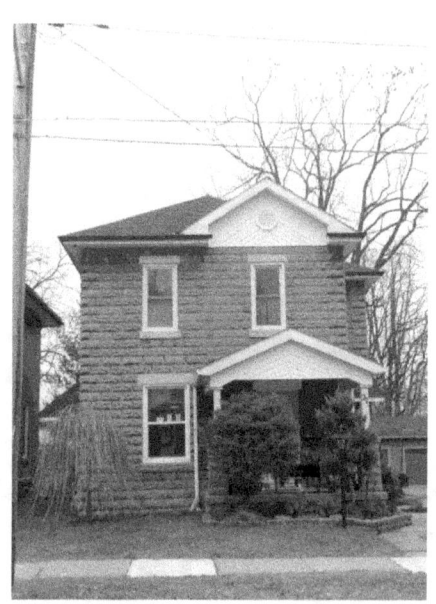

27 Broadway - modernized

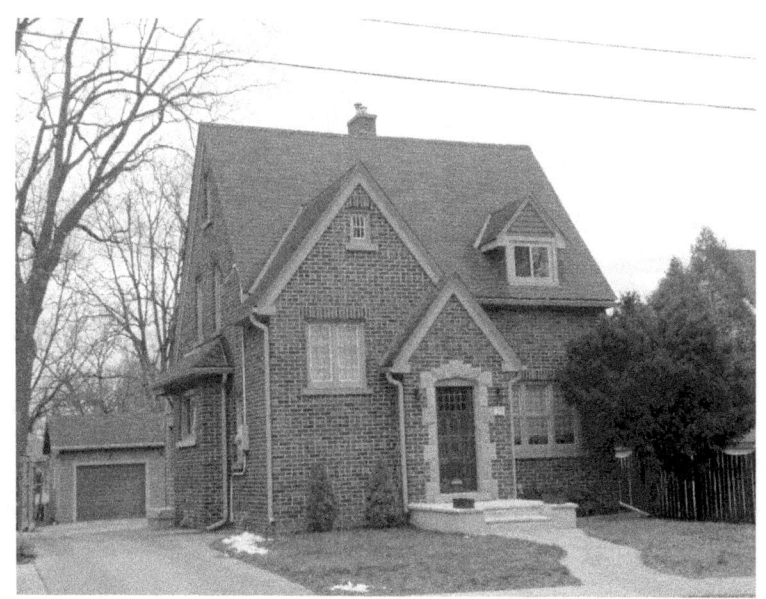

25 Broadway – red brick, quoins around doorway, steeply pitched gable roof

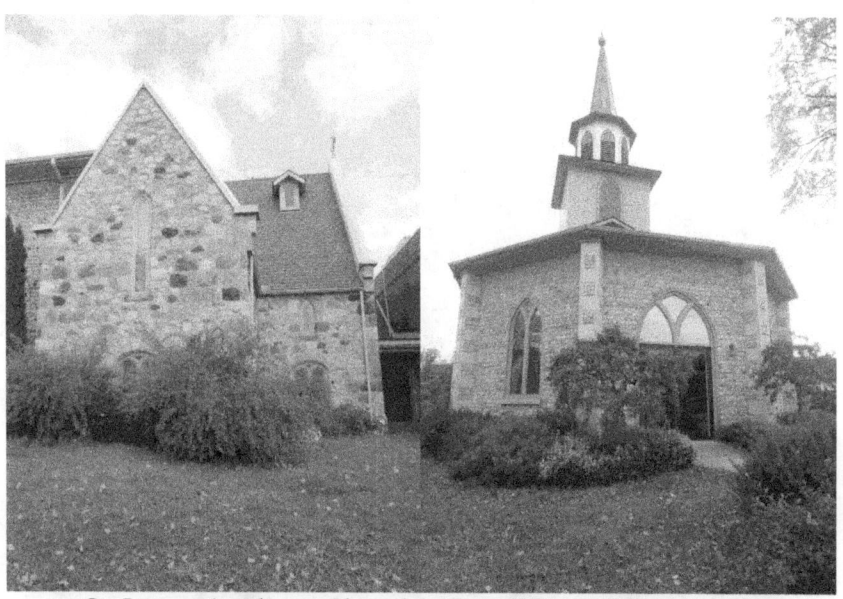

St. James Anglican Church – Grand River Street South
Old part of building, to left, built in 1839 by Levi Broughton, a mason who moved from Normandale, New York and introduced cobblestone-faced masonry. New front section built in 1989.

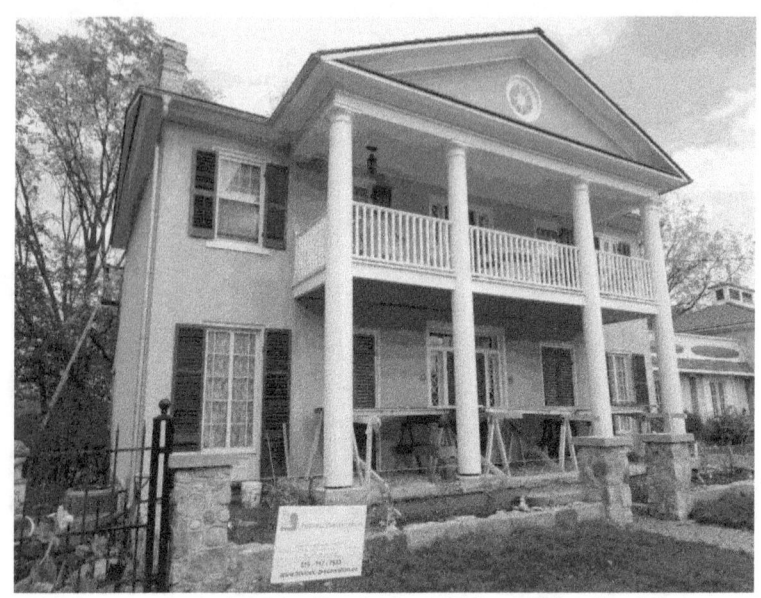

Asa Wolverton settled in Paris in 1832 and built this stuccoed Plantation Manor wood frame house covered in plaster about 1851 in Greek Revival style. Wolverton was a prosperous lumber dealer and contractor - 52 Grand River Street South

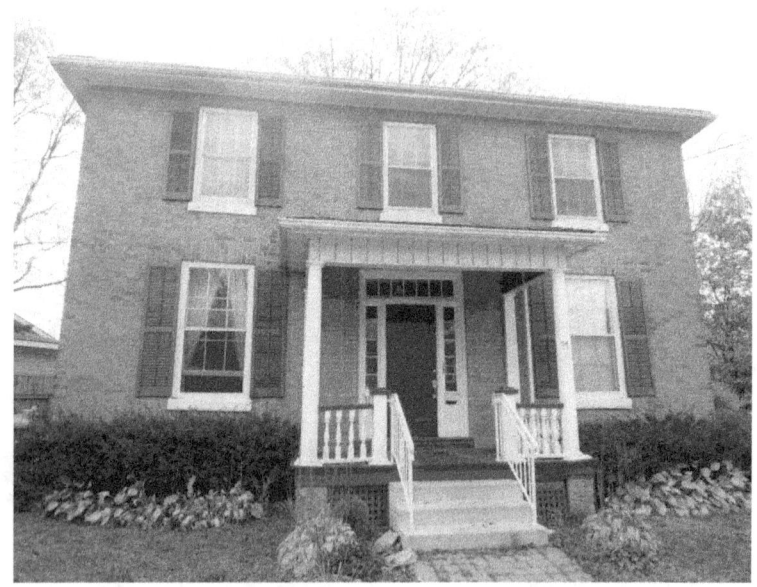

31 Grand River Street South – Georgian style, red-orange brick

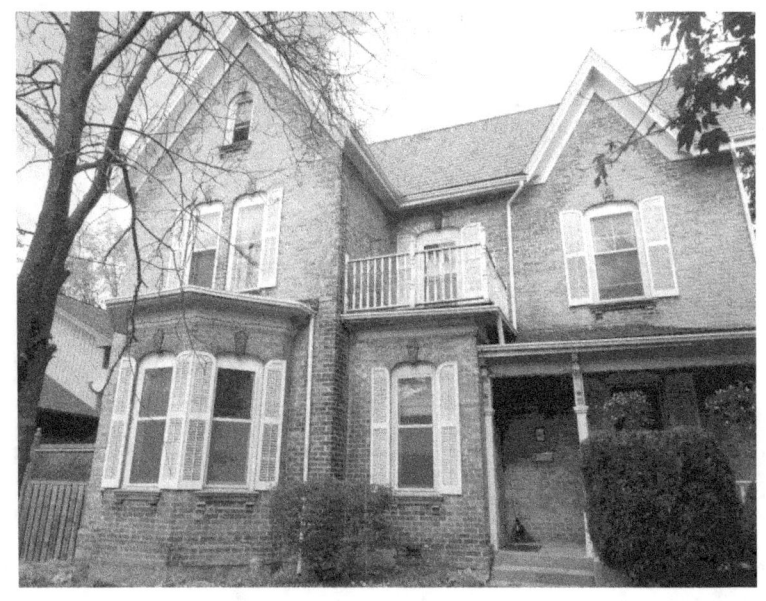

40 Grand River Street South – Gothic Revival style
Yellow-brown brick, bay window, balcony on second storey

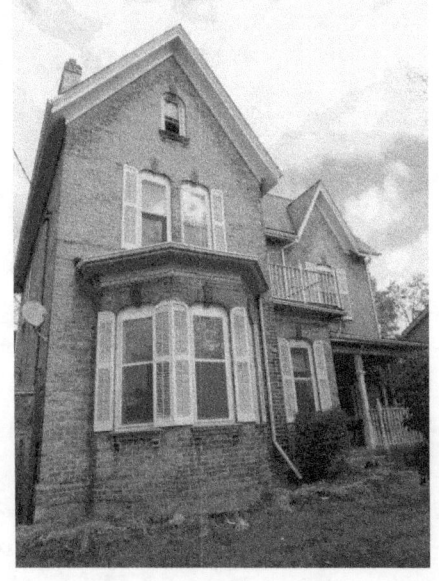

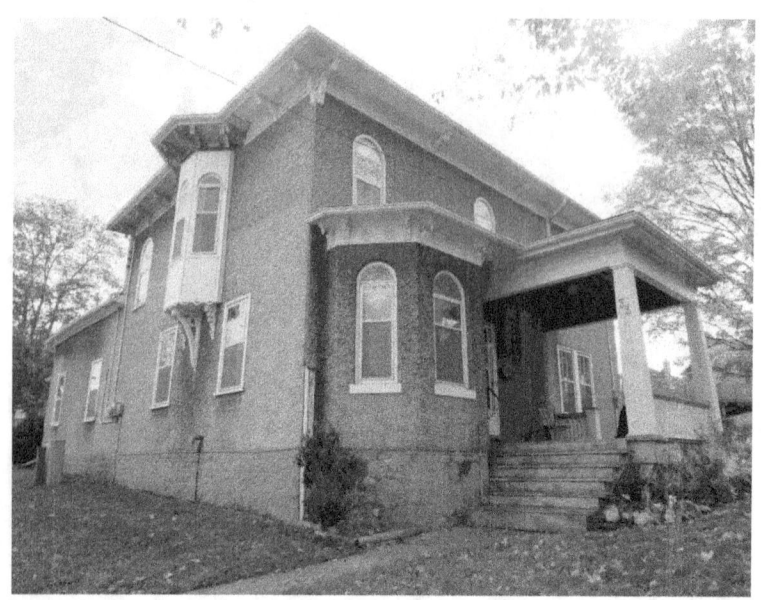

33 Grand River Street South – Italianate style – stucco exterior

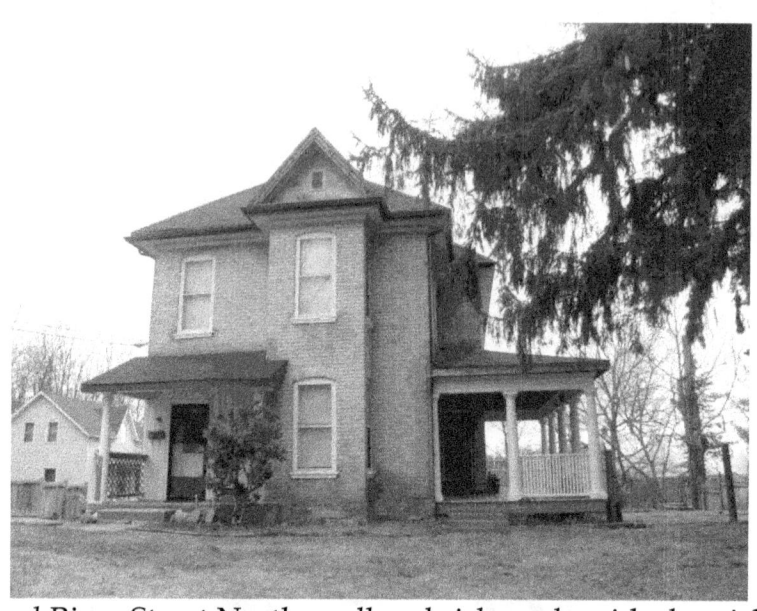

Grand River Street North - yellow brick made with clay rich in lime

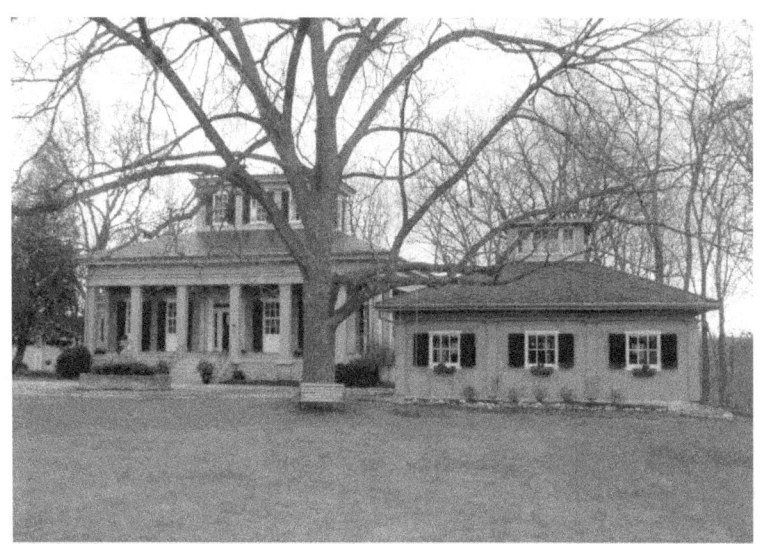

165 Grand River Street North – built and occupied by Norman Hamilton, a wealthy local industrialist, miller and brewer; a three-storey cobblestone building designed in the Greek Revival style c. 1839-1844 – it appears to be 1½ storeys in height – the second storey windows are set in light-wells in the verandah roof and are concealed from view by the deep architrave of the verandah. The pillars are square; triple hung windows on the first and third floors.

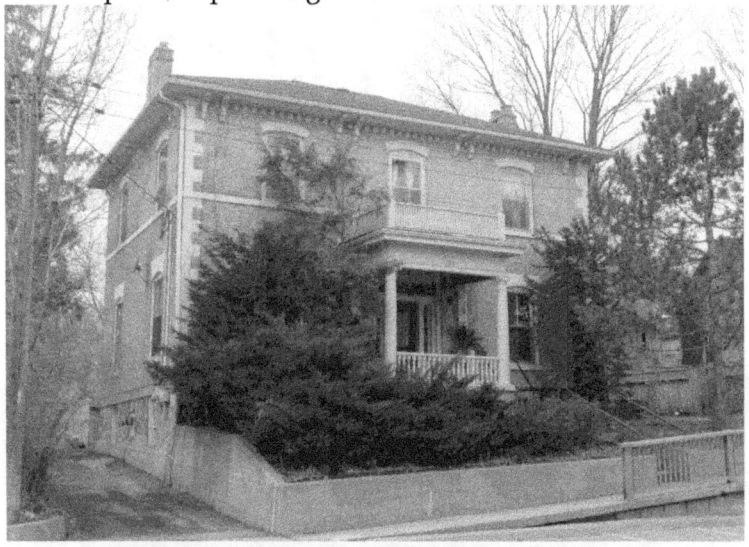

174 Grand River Street North - Italianate

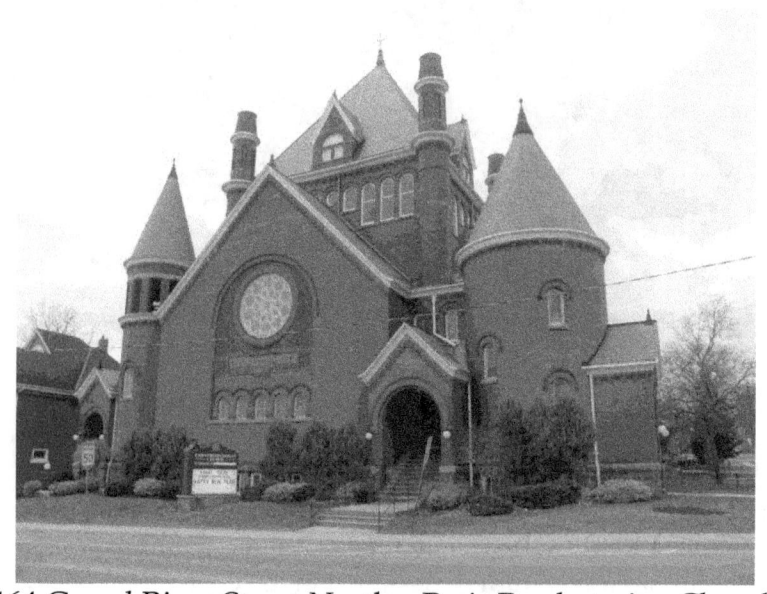

164 Grand River Street North – Paris Presbyterian Church
Red brick, turrets, conical towers

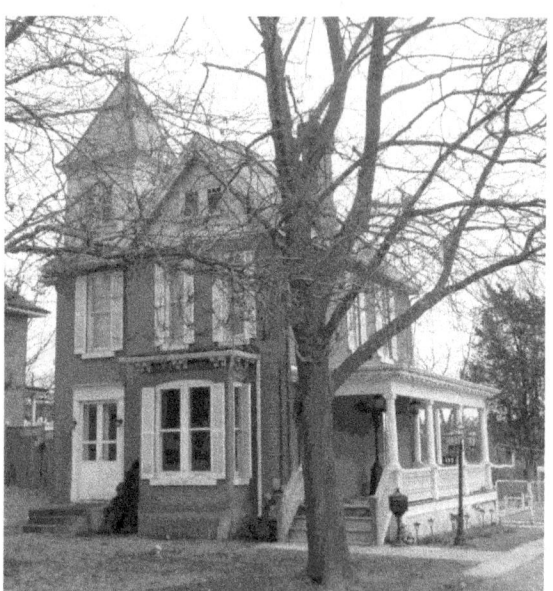

173 Grand River Street North

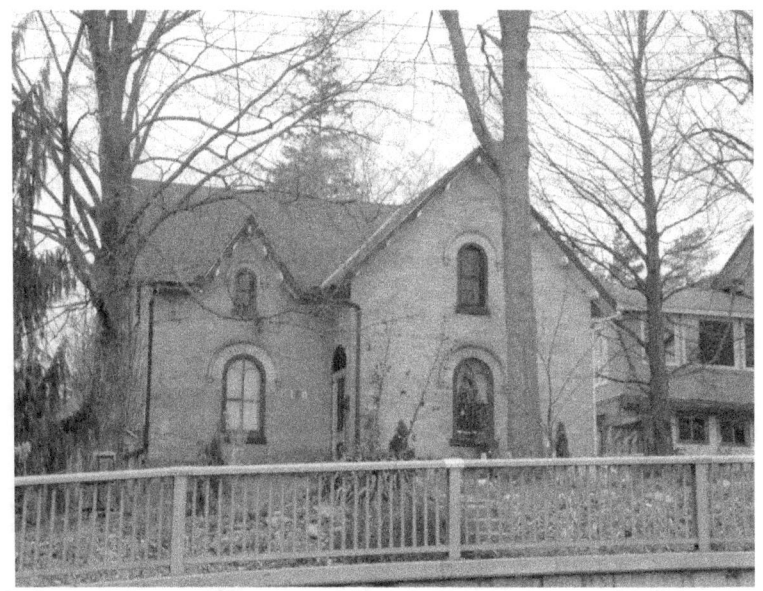

180 Grand River Street North – decorative window voussoirs

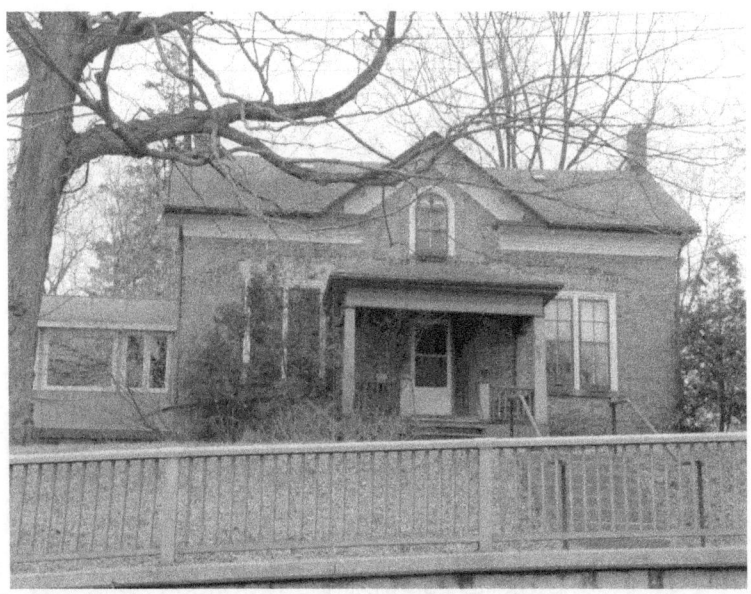

182 Grand River Street North – Gothic cottage – yellow brick

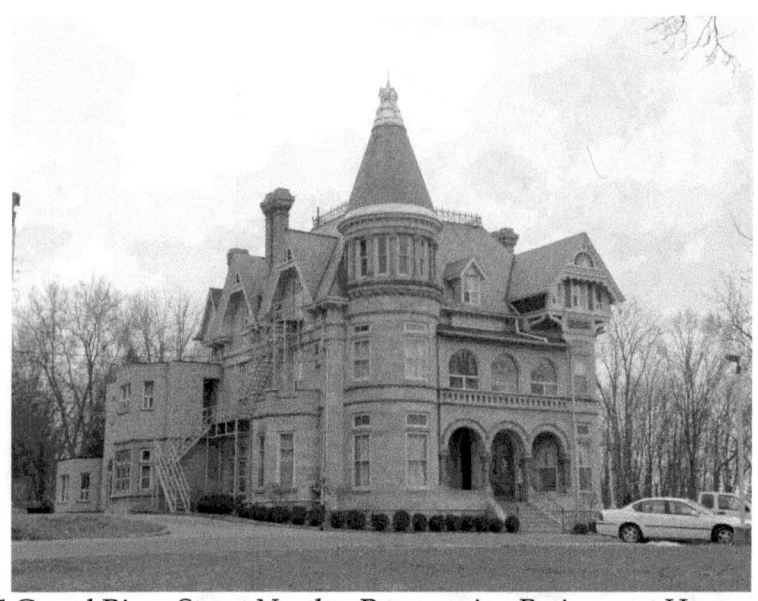

185 Grand River Street North – Penmarvian Retirement Home was built in 1845 by the founder of Paris, Hiram Capron, as a modest two storey building. In 1887 local industrialist John Penman purchased the home and added the turrets, towers and arches.

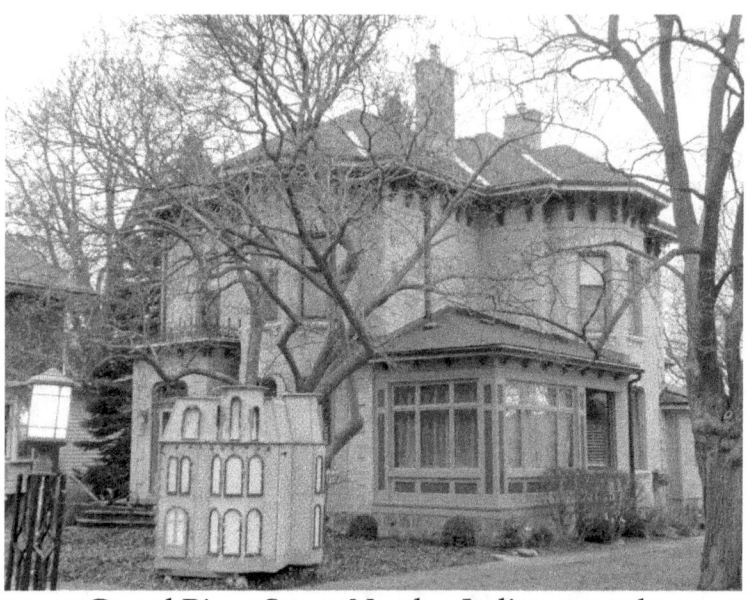

Grand River Street North – Italianate style

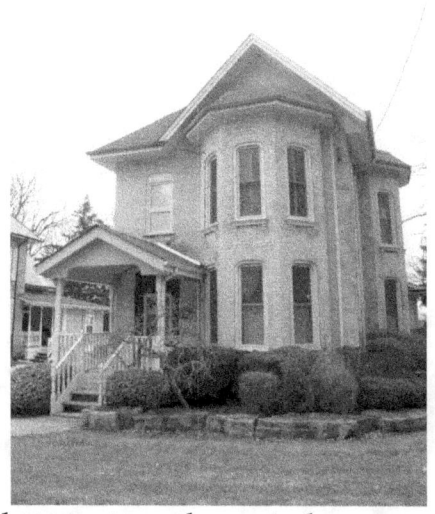

Yellow brick, two storey bay window, round windows

Grand River Street North

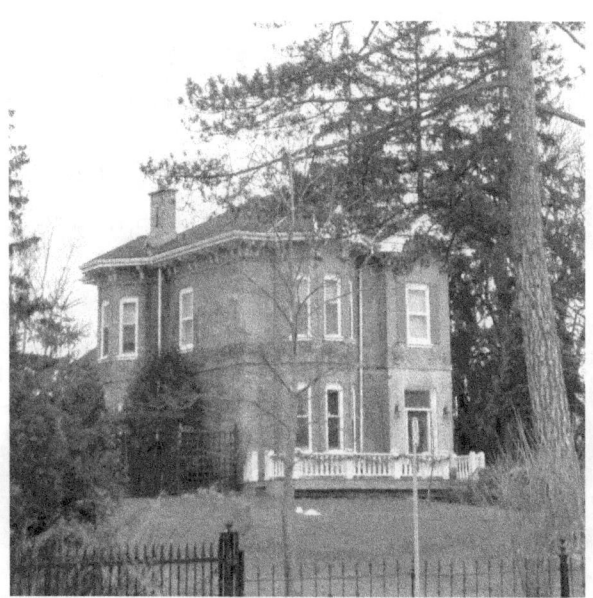

Italianate style

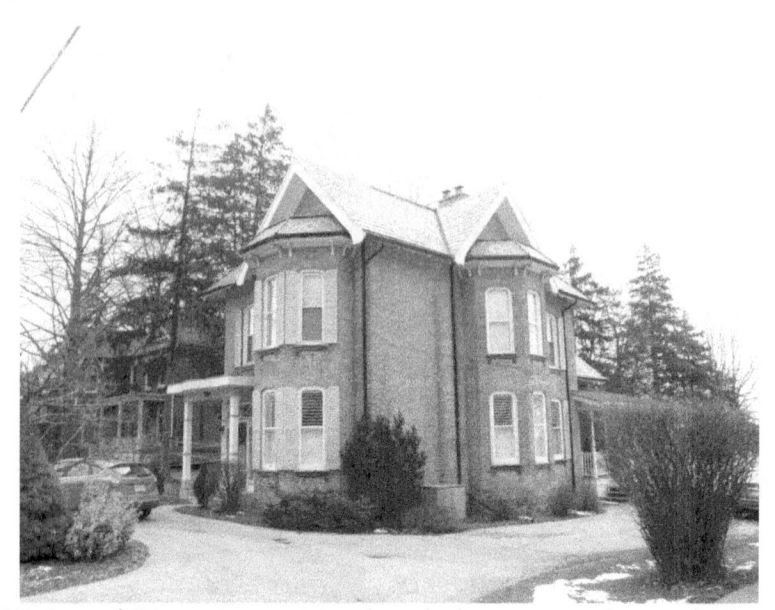

197 Grand River Street North – dichromatic tile work above two-storey bay windows

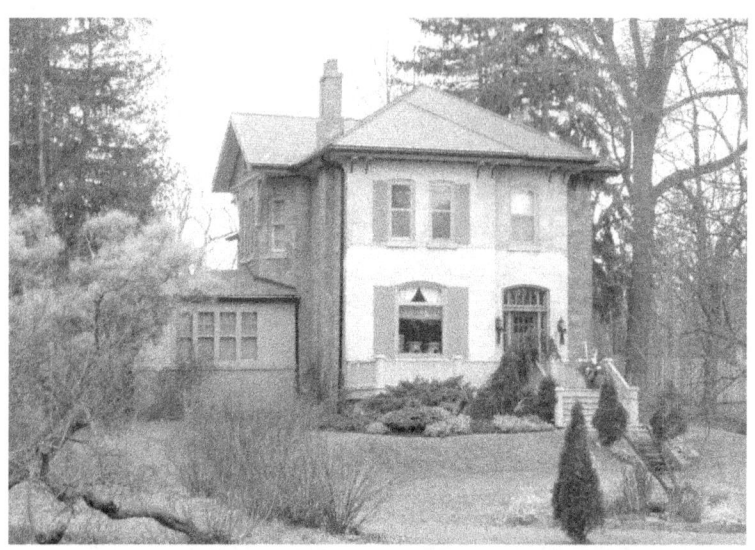

20_ Grand River Street North – yellow brick

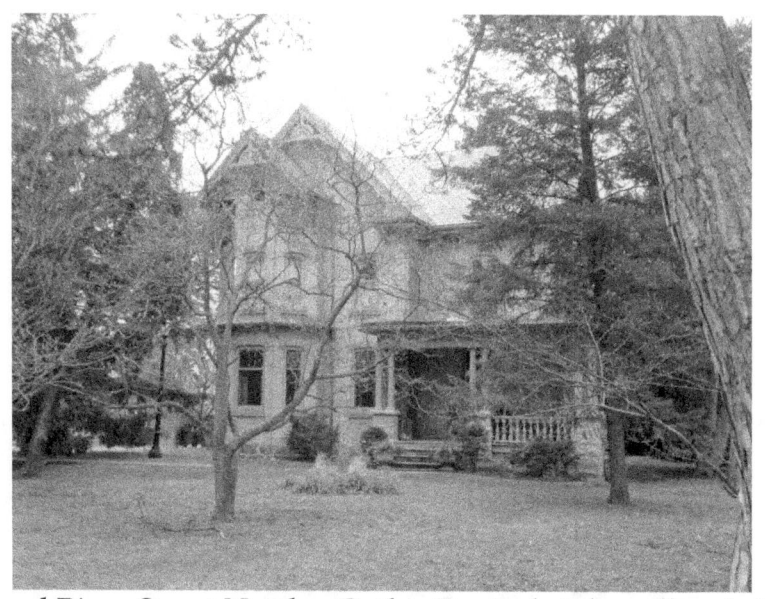

Grand River Street North – Gothic Revival style, yellow brick, two-storey bay window

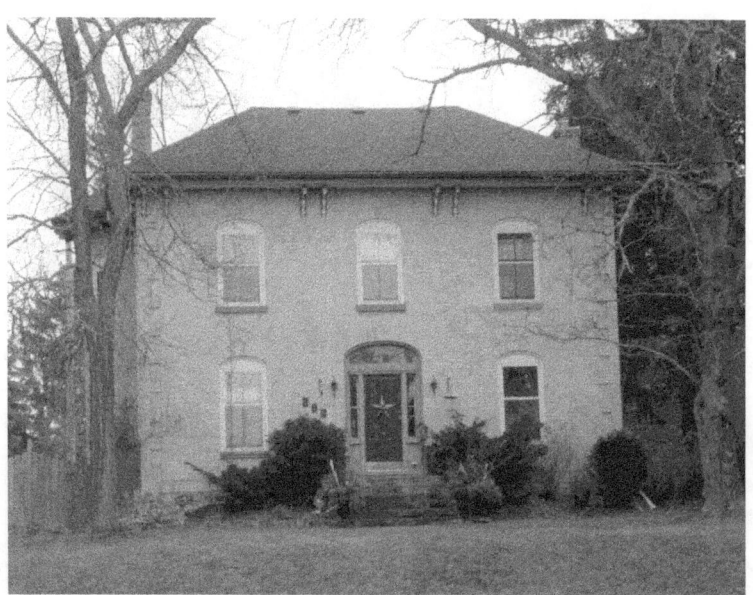

204 Grand River Street North – Italianate style – paired cornice brackets, yellow brick, quoins on corners

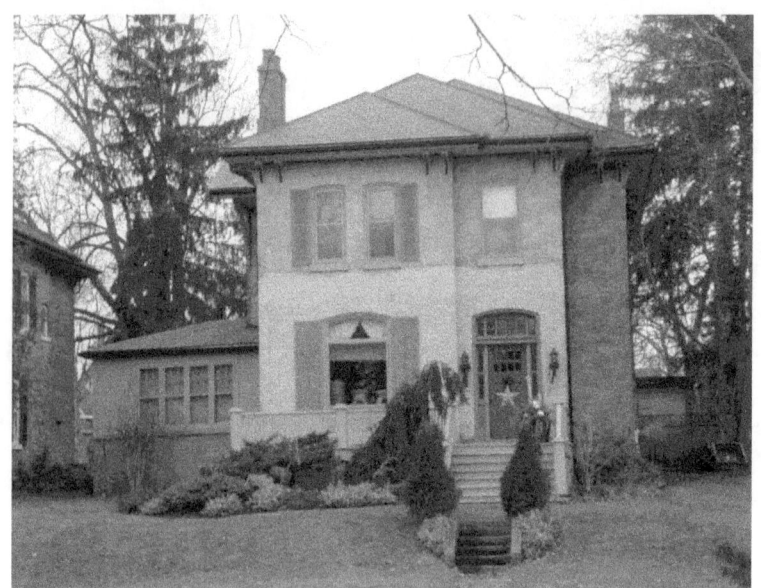

202 Grand River Street North – Italianate, yellow brick

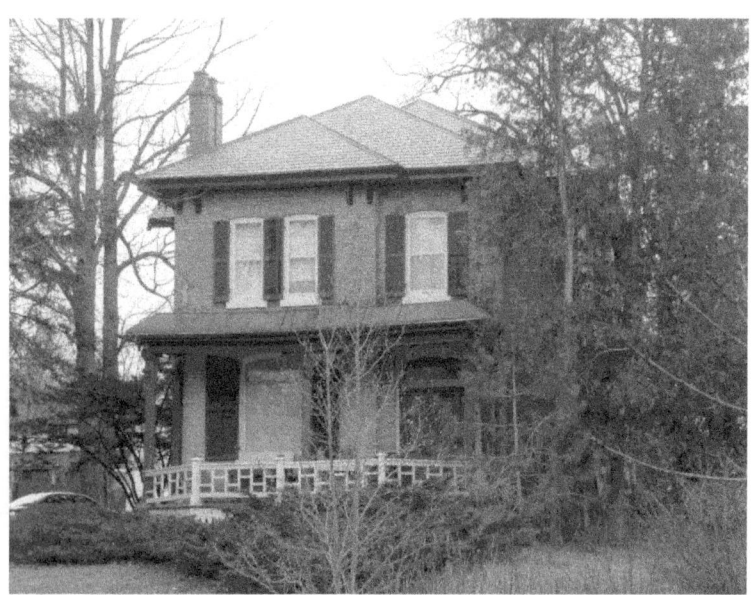

Grand River Street North – yellow brick, triple level roof

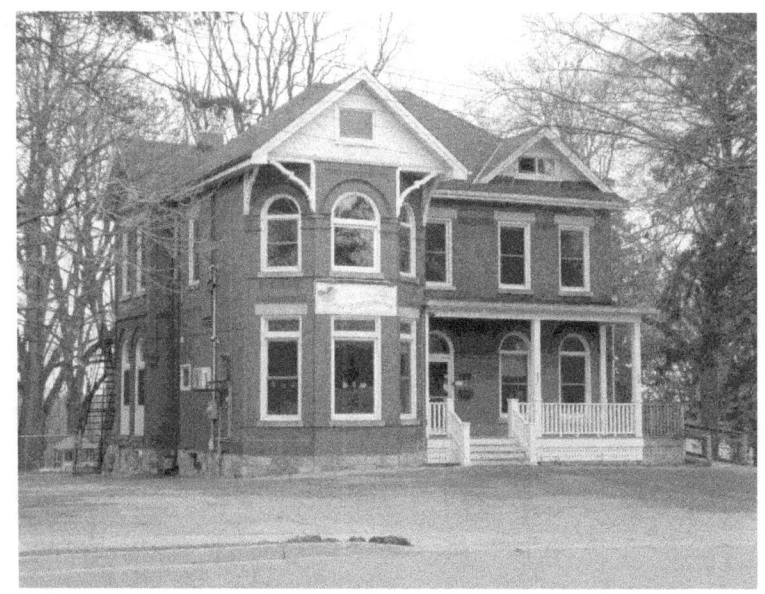

199 Grand River Street North – red brick – Edwardian style

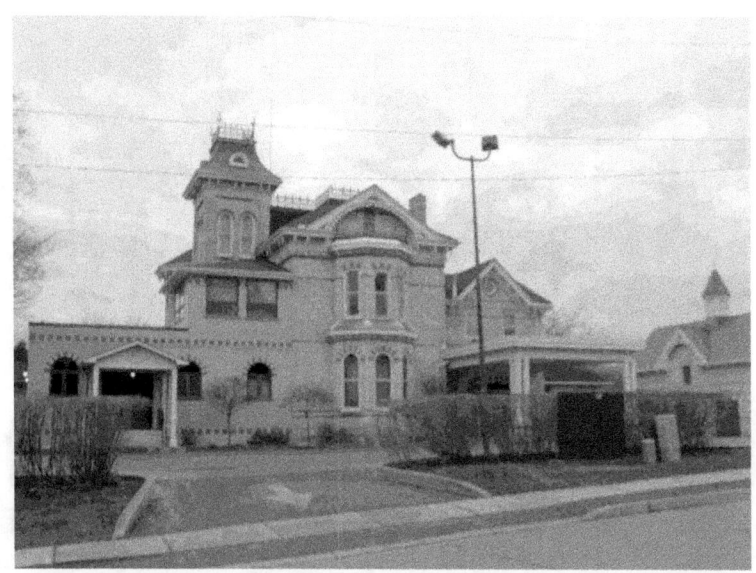

184 Grand River Street North – Queen Anne style

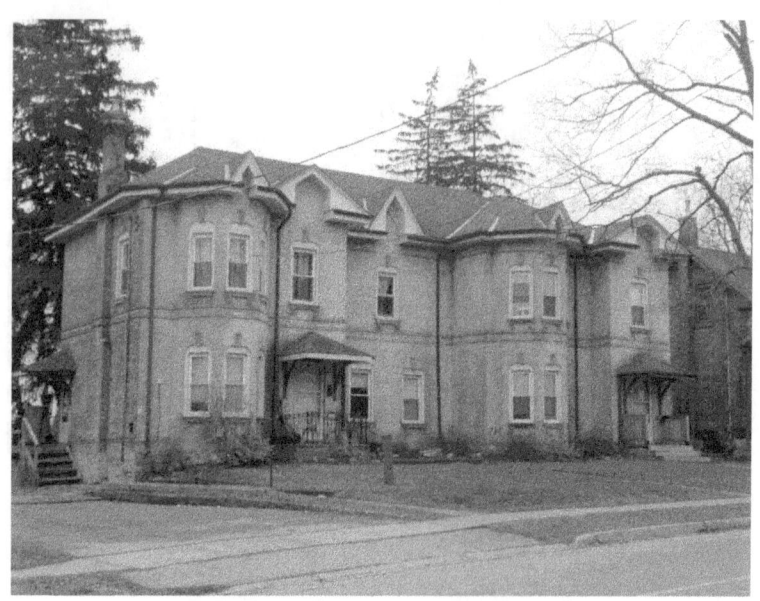

145 Grand River Street North

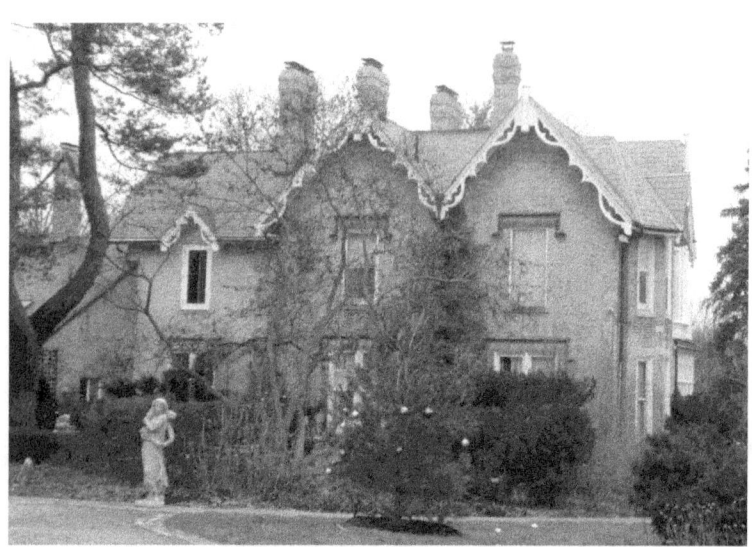

Grand River Street North – Gothic Revival, decorative Vergeboard on gables

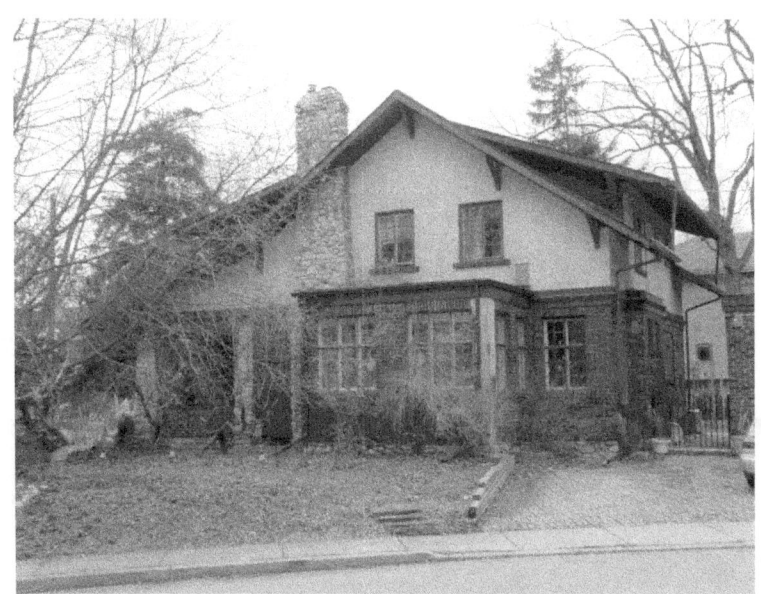

Stucco exterior on second storey, cobblestone chimney

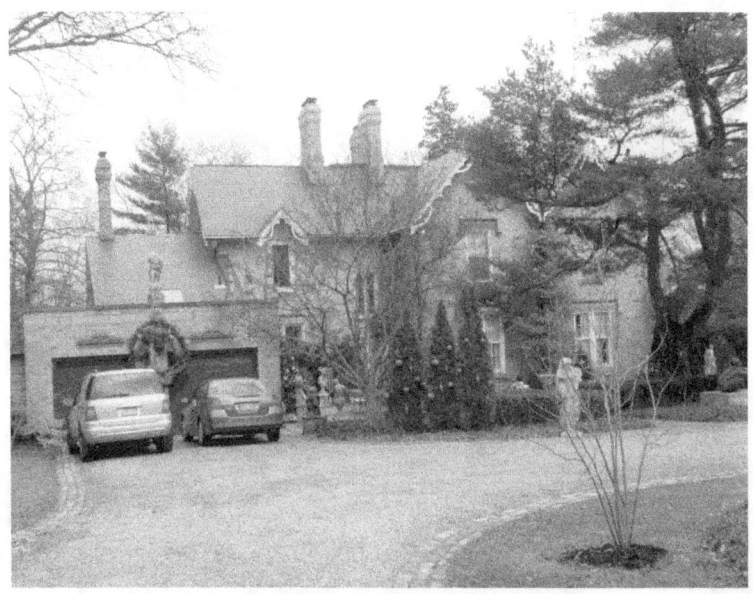

Gothic Revival

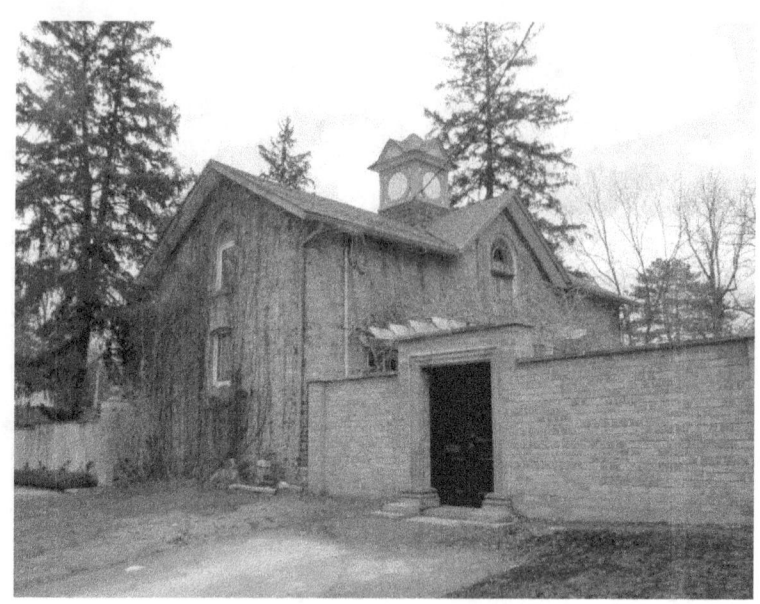
18 – Wisteria Cottage

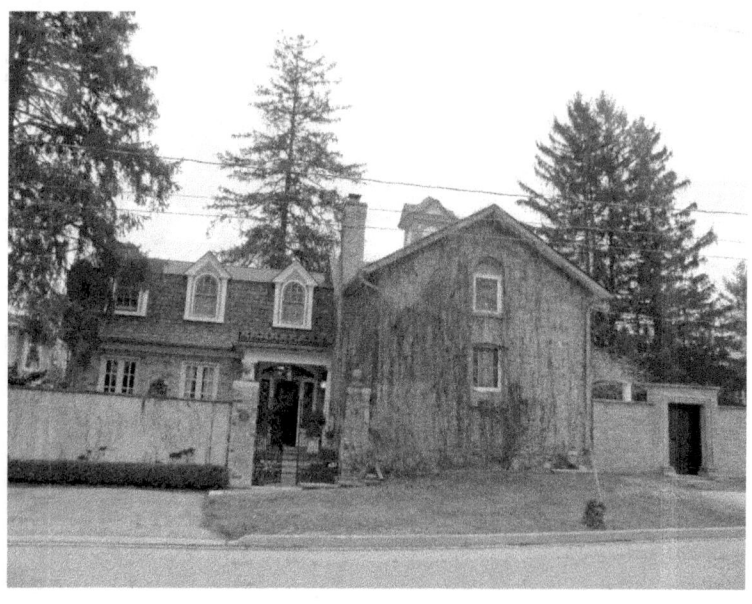

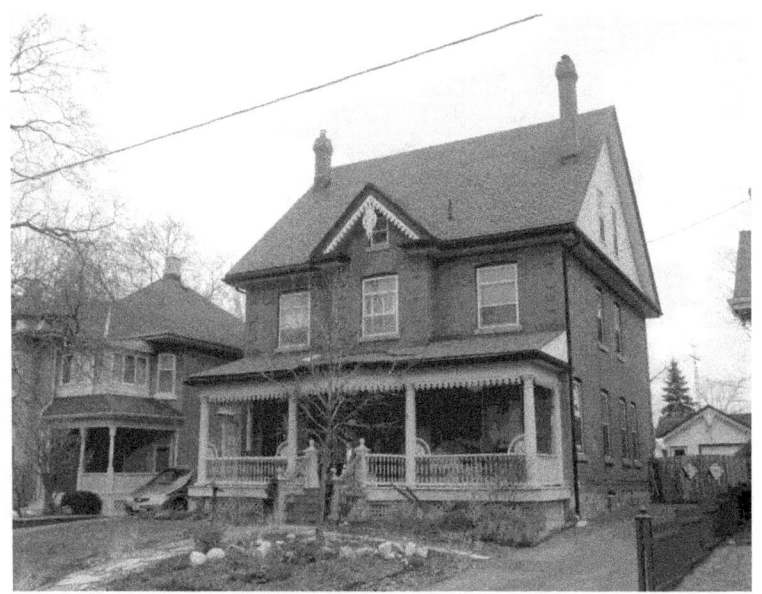

15 Jane Street – Gothic Revival style – Vergeboard trim on gable, central frontispiece facade

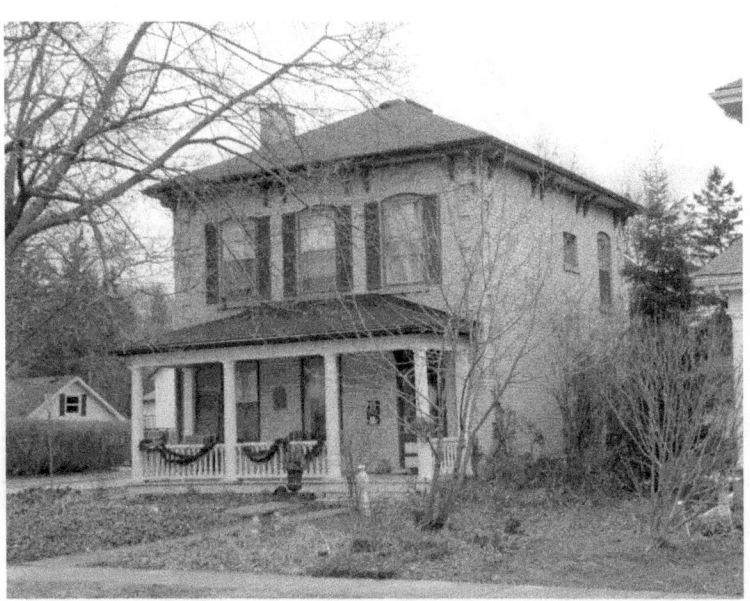

Jane Street – Italianate style – paired cornice brackets, hip roof

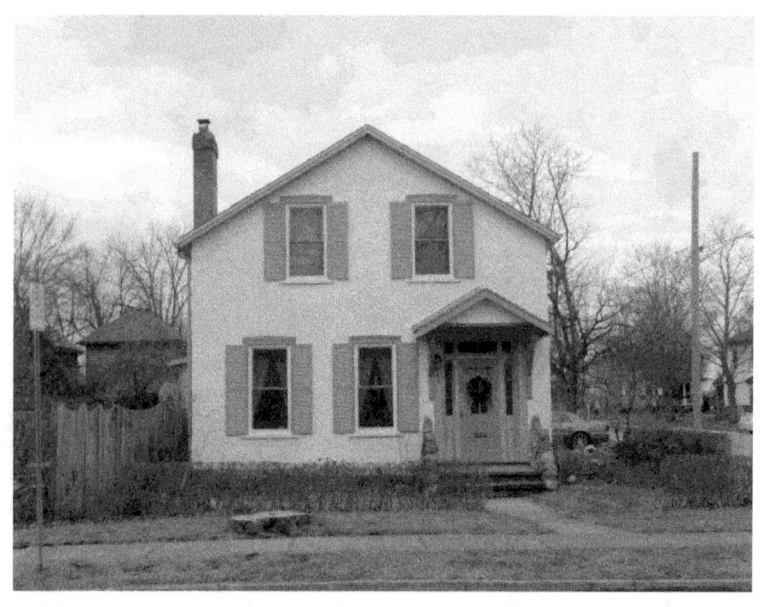

24 Jane Street – 1½ storey Gothic Cottage with stucco exterior

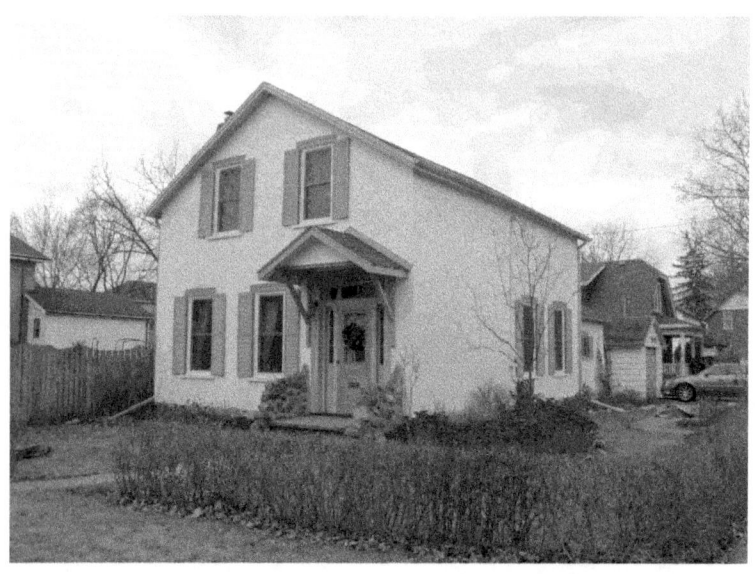

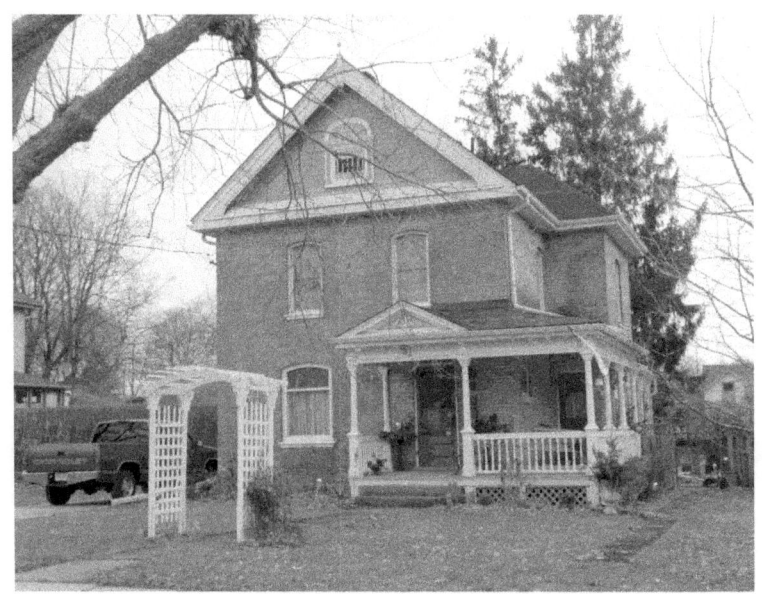

31 Jane Street – Edwardian style

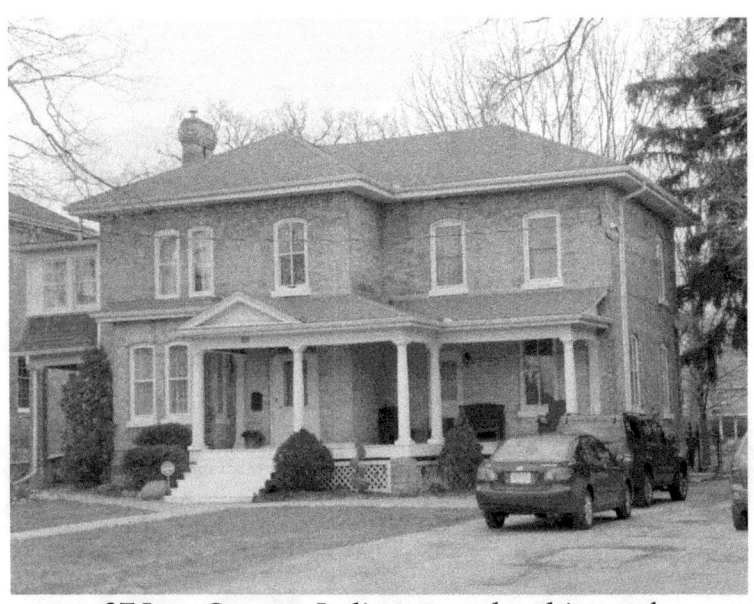

37 Jane Street – Italianate style – hip roof

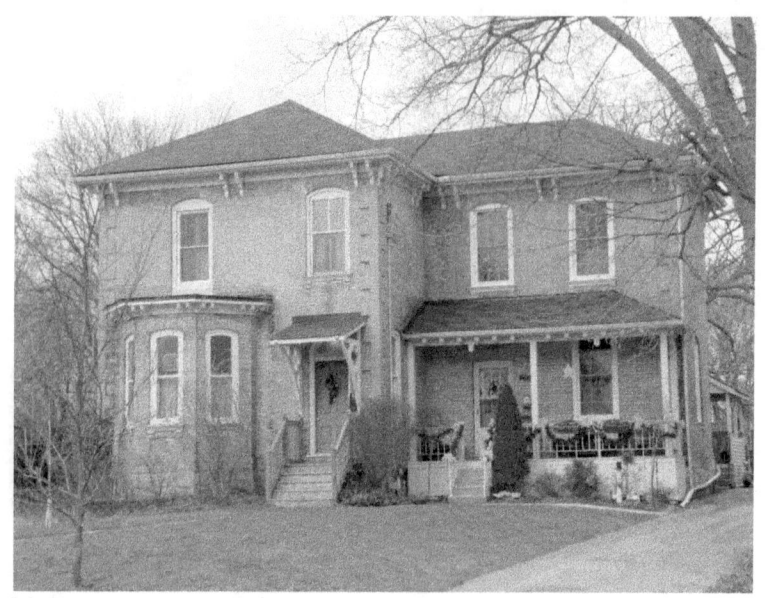

39 Jane Street – Italianate – paired cornice brackets, bay window

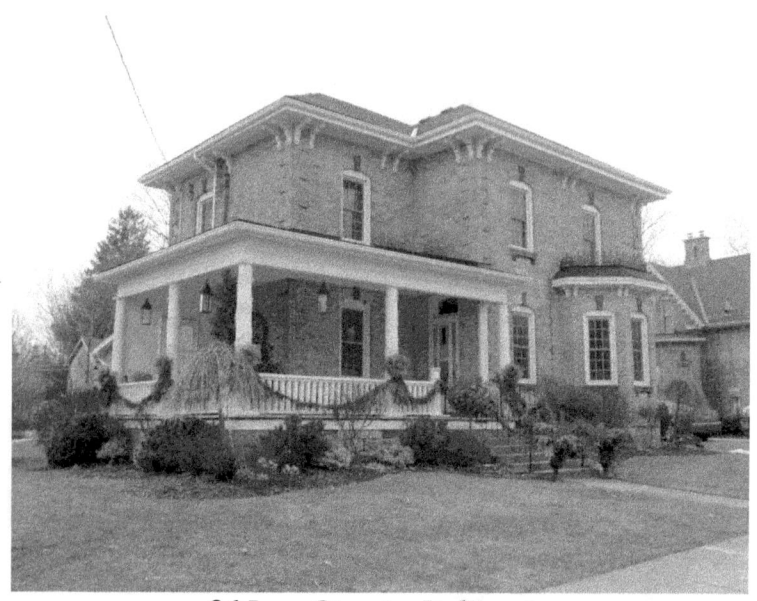

36 Jane Street – Italianate

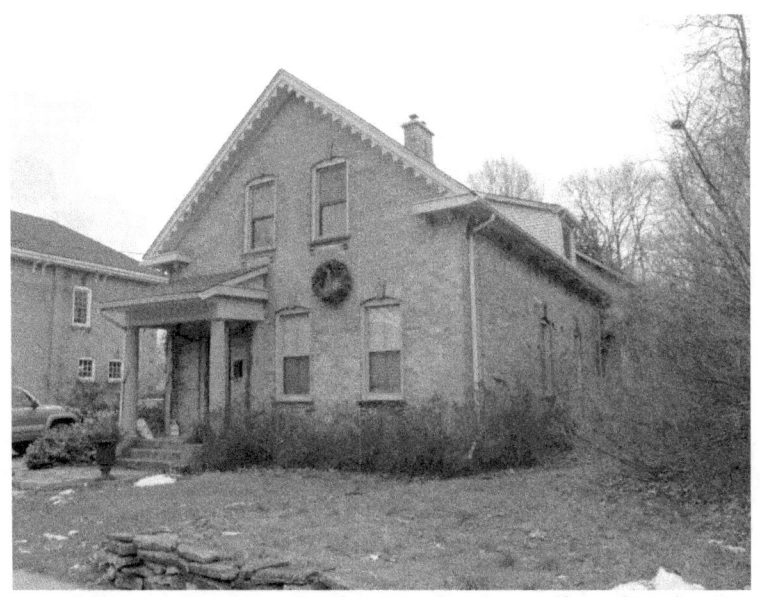

38 Jane Street – Gothic Revival – yellow brick

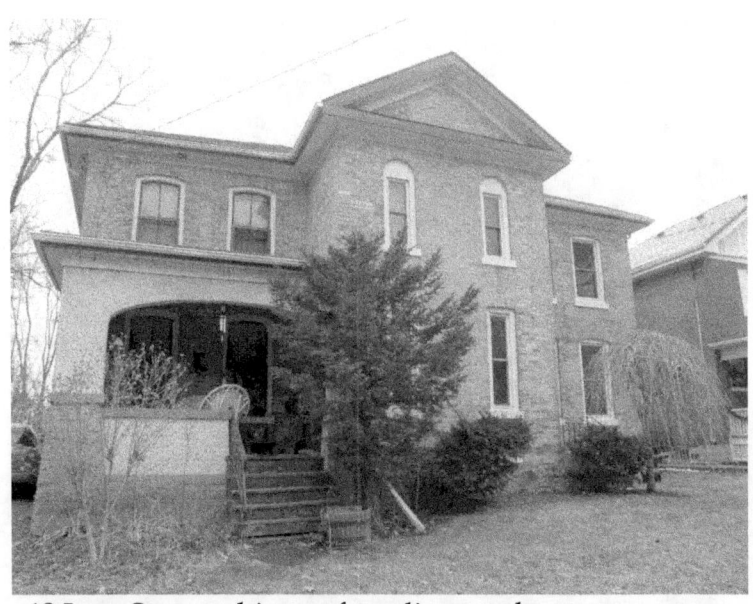

40 Jane Street – hip roof, pediment above two-storey projecting wall

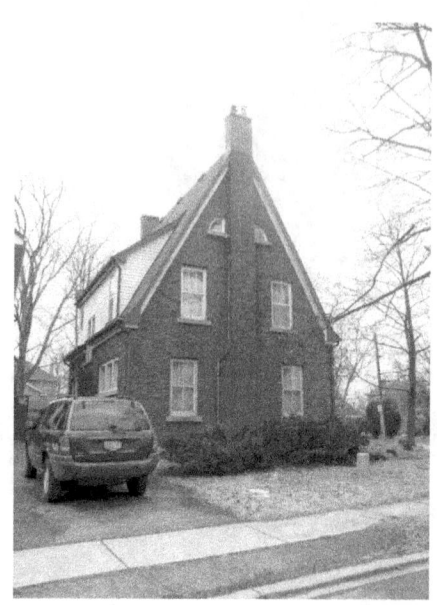

Jane Street – 2½ storey house, very steep gable

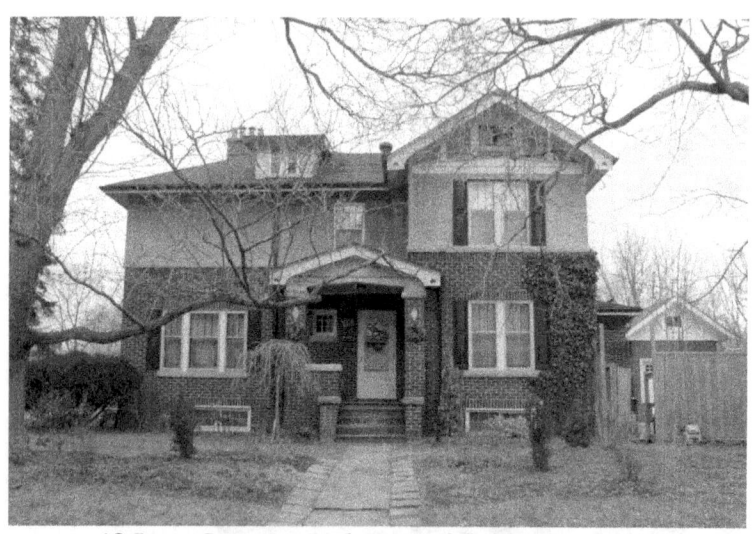

49 Jane Street – Italianate/Gothic mixture

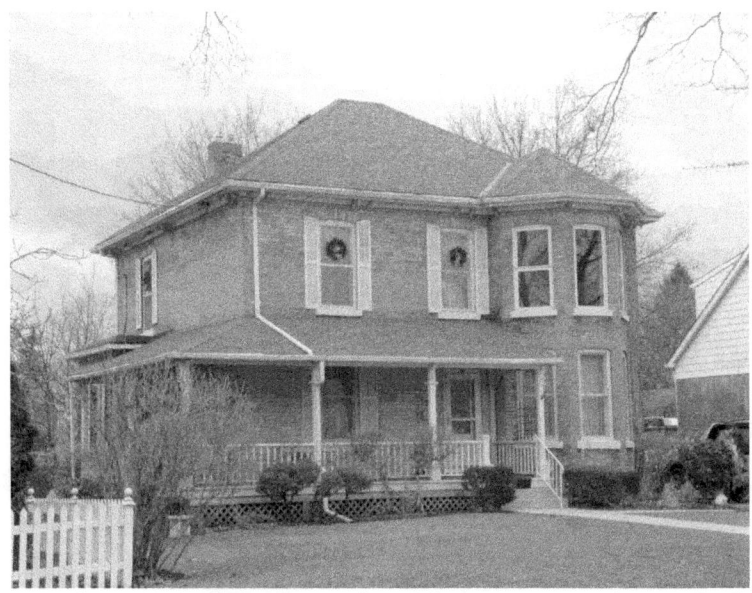

13 Jane Street – Italianate style with two-storey bay window, paired cornice brackets, yellow brick

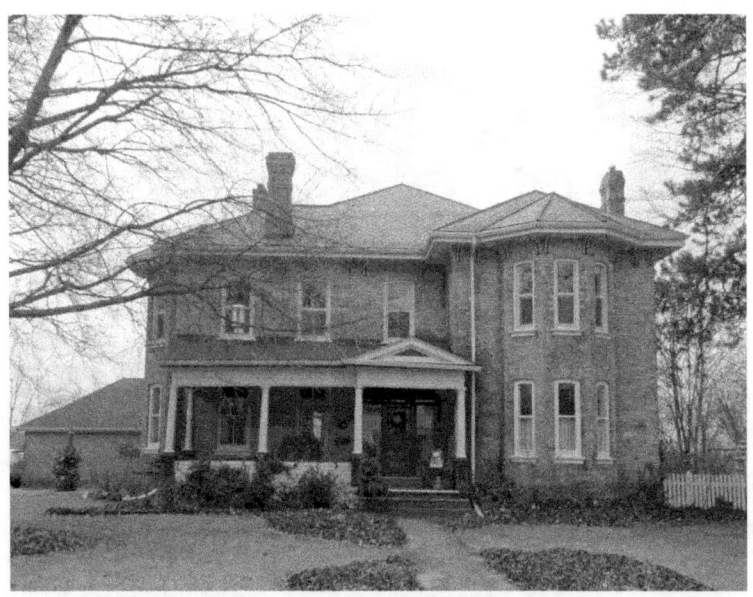

50 Jane Street – similar style to the one above

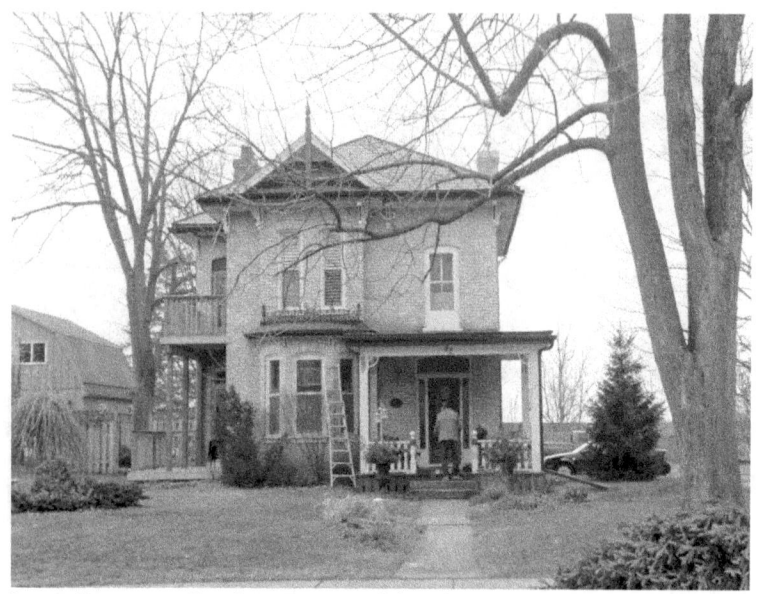

48 Jane Street – Gothic Revival/Italianate – gable with finial, cornice brackets, bay windows with iron cresting above

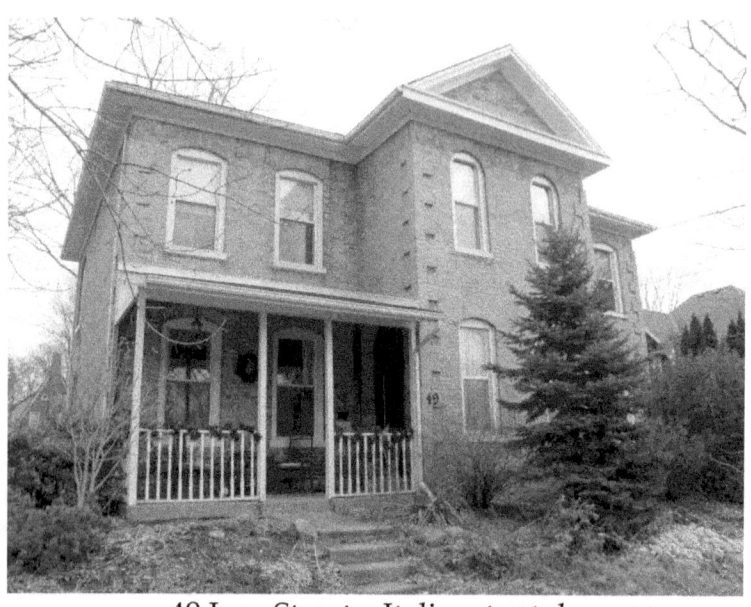

49 Jane Street – Italianate style

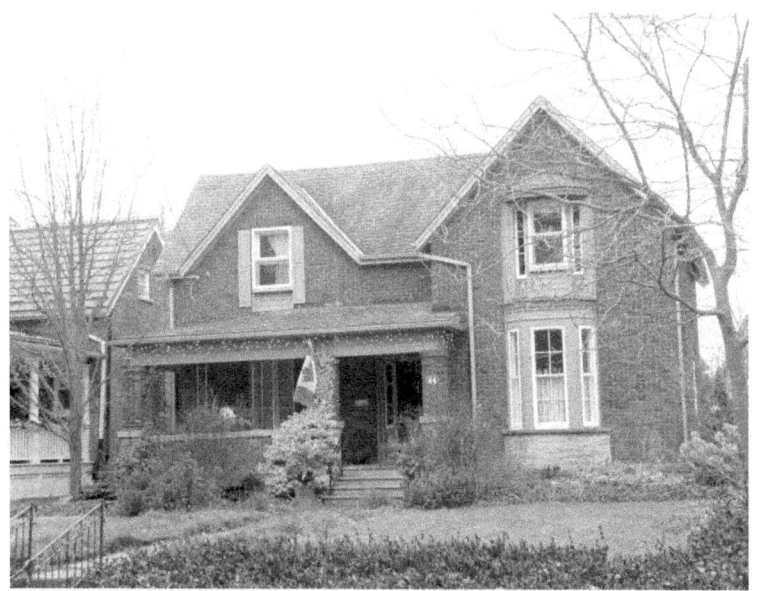

44 Banfield Street – Gothic Revival with two-storey bay windows, red brick

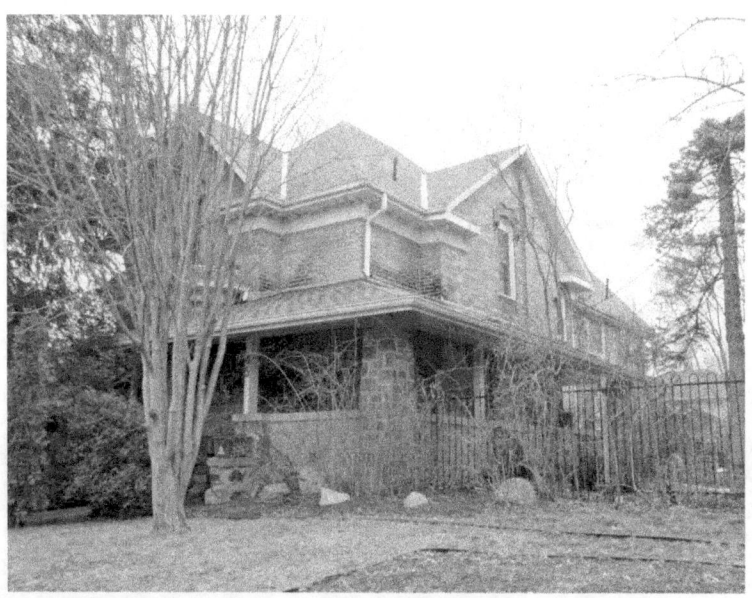

Banfield Street – Gothic Revival/Queen Anne mixture – yellow brick

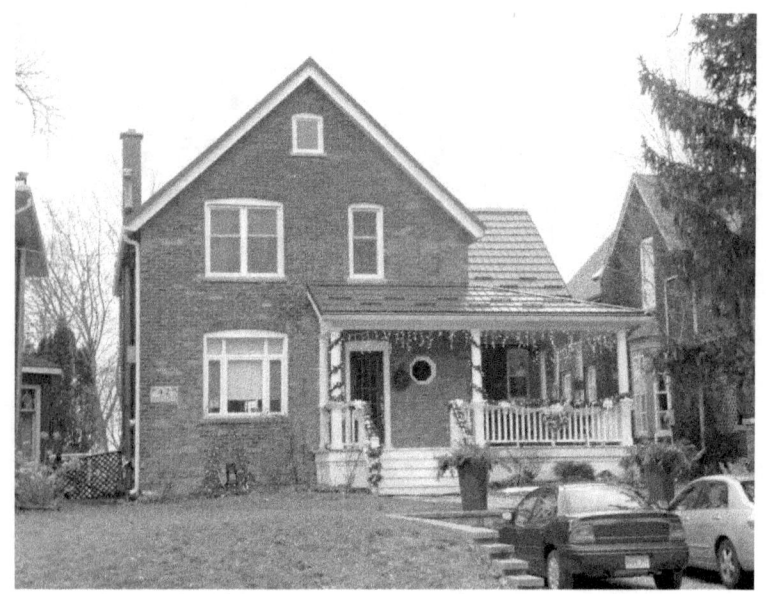

42 Banfield Street – Gothic Revival, red brick

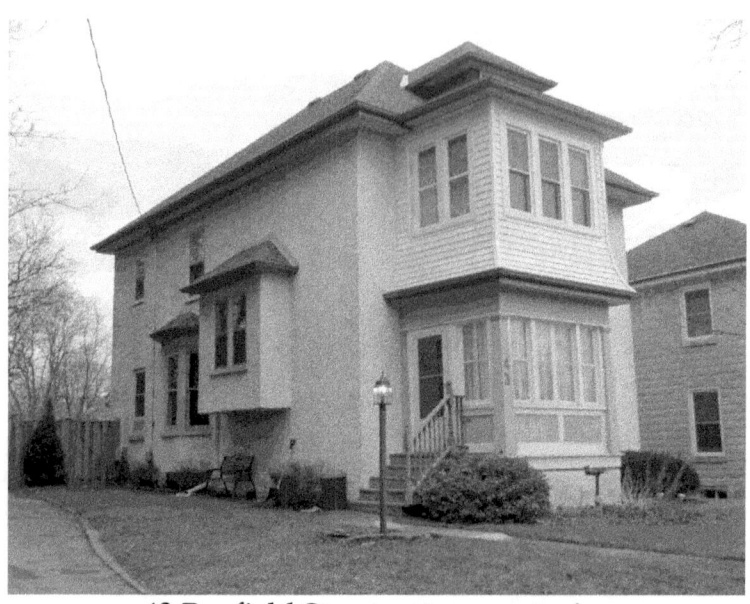

43 Banfield Street – stucco exterior

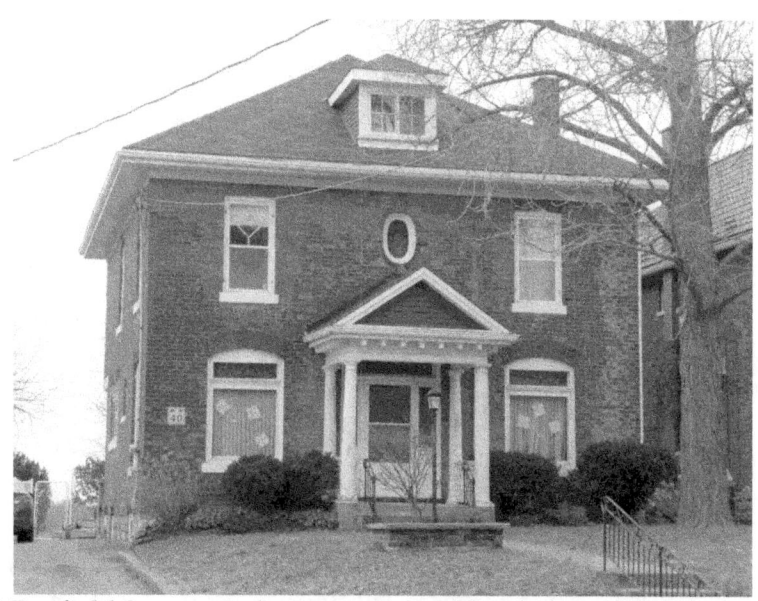

40 Banfield Street – Italianate style, red brick, frontispiece around centre doorway, round window in centre of second storey, dormer in the attic

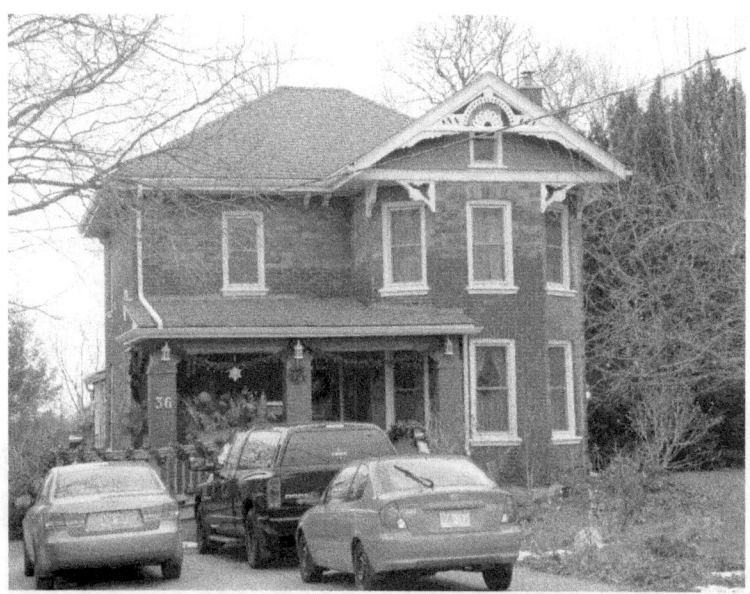

36 Banfield Street – Italianate/Gothic Revival – hip roof, cornice brackets, two-storey bay window with decorative Vergeboard on gable, voussoirs above windows

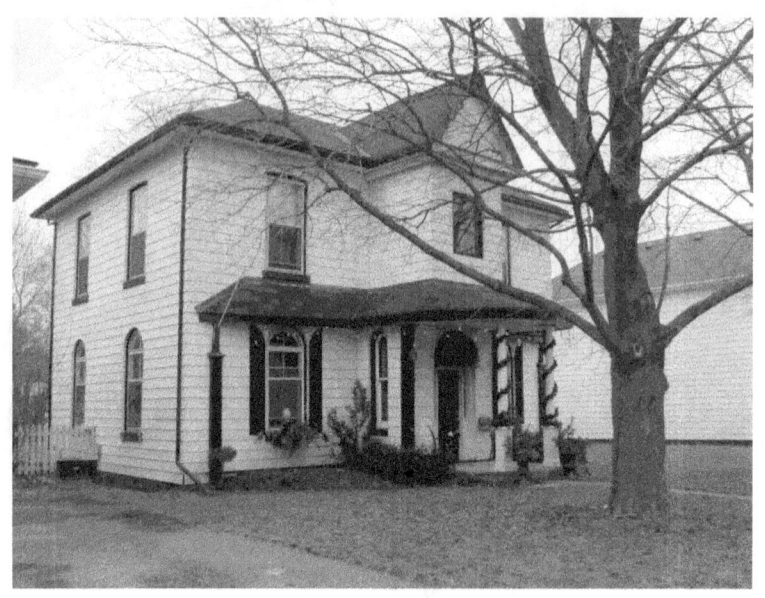

Banfield Street

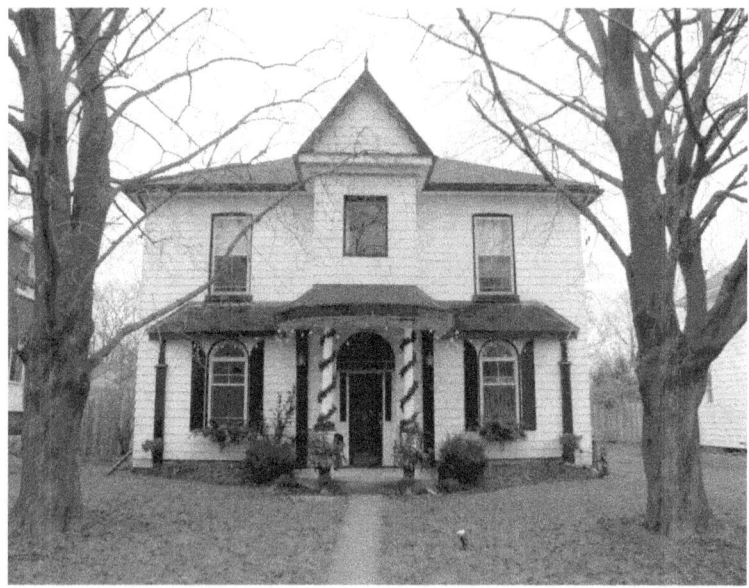

Italianate with two-storey frontispiece topped by a gable with decorative vergeboards and finial

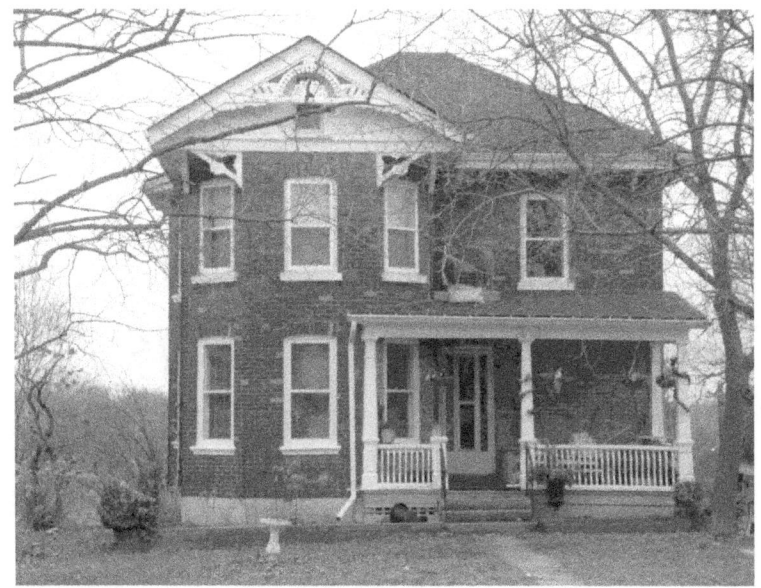

Banfield Street – Gothic Revival/Italianate – decorative Vergeboard, cornice brackets

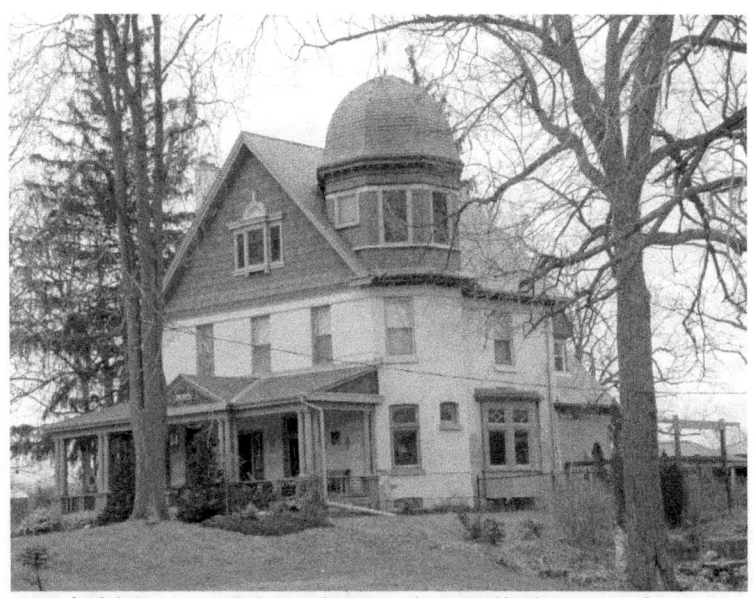

18 Banfield Street – Edwardian style – Palladian window, turret extending through the roof

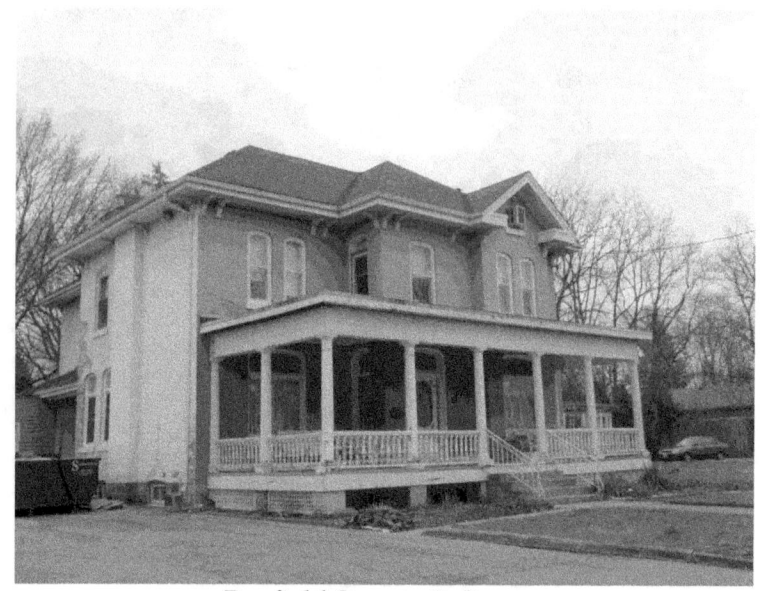

Banfield Street - Italianate

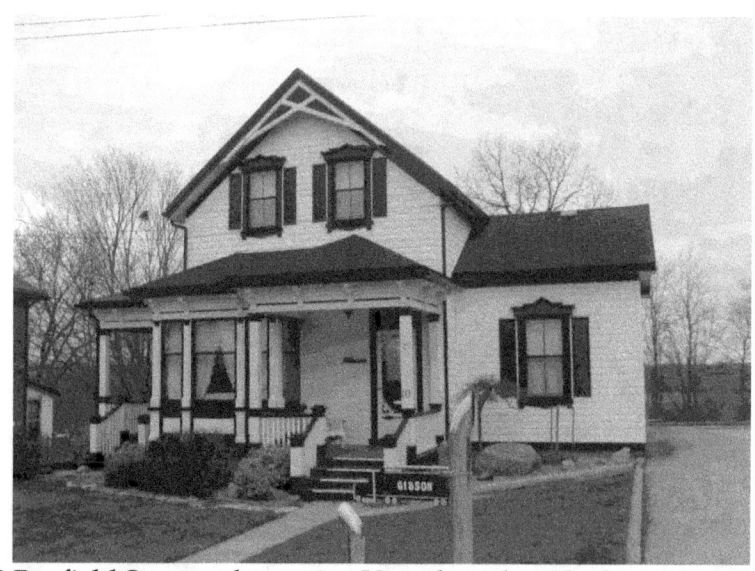

10 Banfield Street – decorative Vergeboard on Gothic style gable, Italianate style veranda with cornice brackets

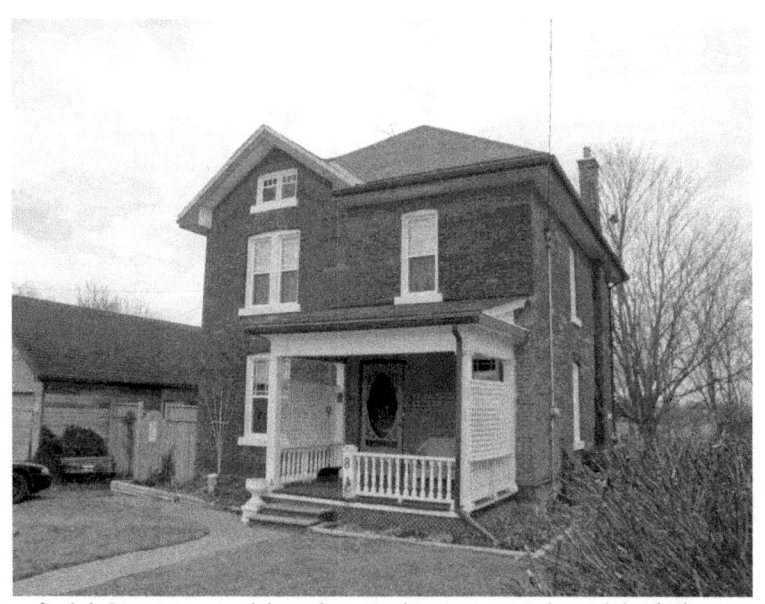

8 Banfield Street – red brick – Italianate with gabled dormer in attic

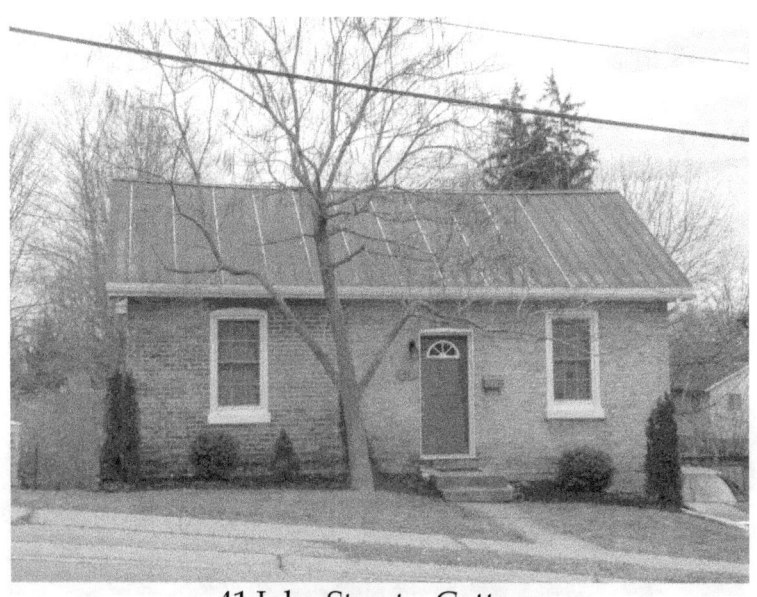

41 John Street – Cottage

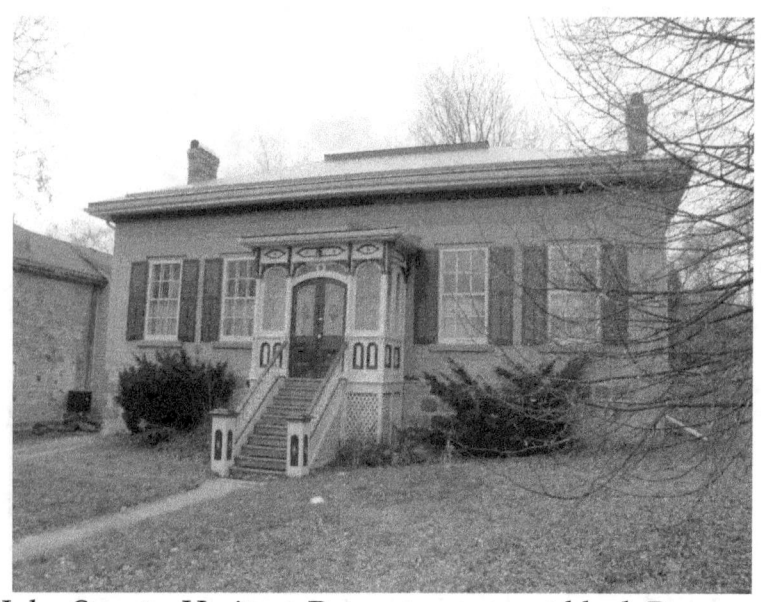

John Street – Heritage Property – cement block Regency Cottage, hip roof, window shutters, decorative enclosed porch

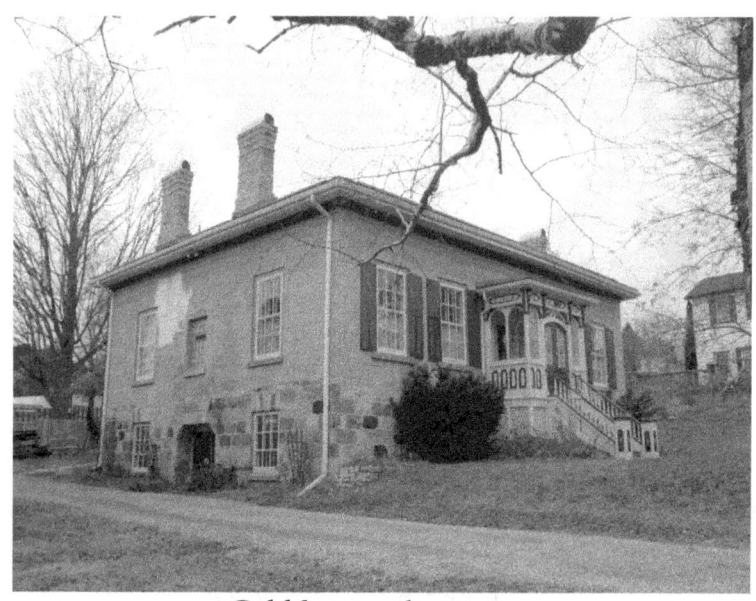

Cobblestone basement

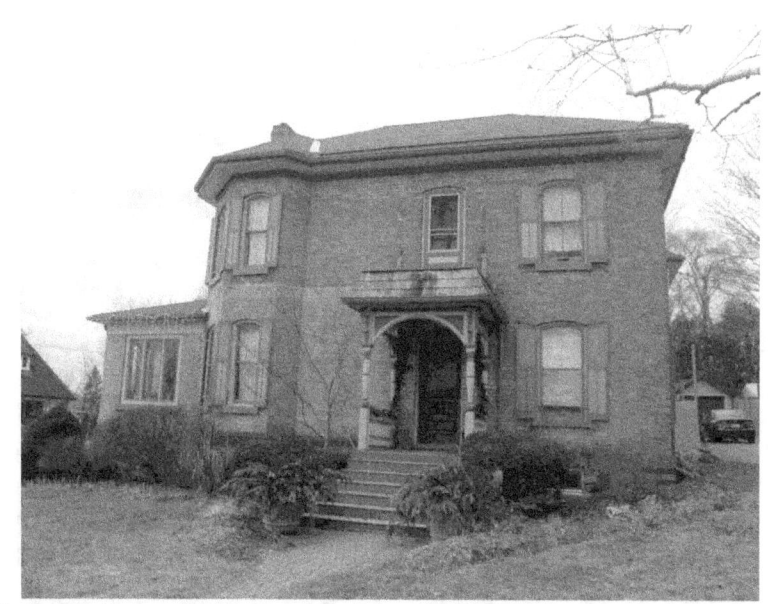

John Street – Italianate style, yellow brick, two-storey bay window

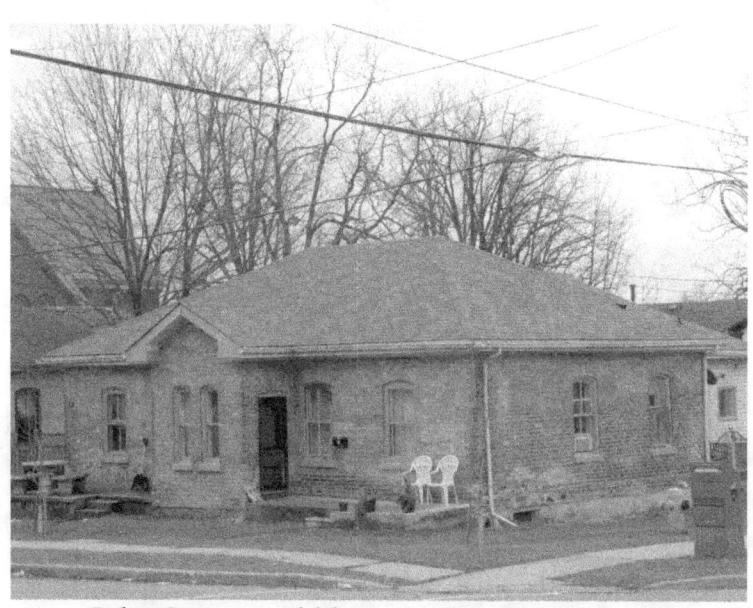

John Street - cobblestone Cottage, hip roof

Glen Morris

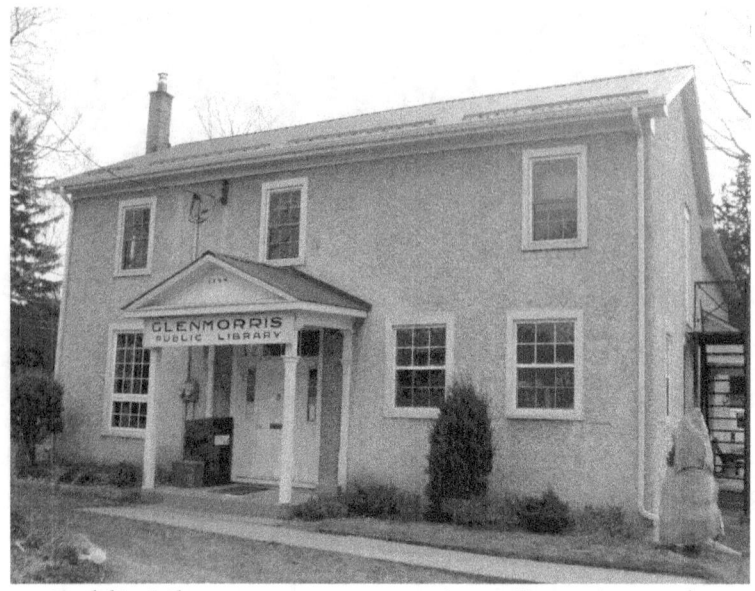

Public Library – stucco exterior – Georgian style

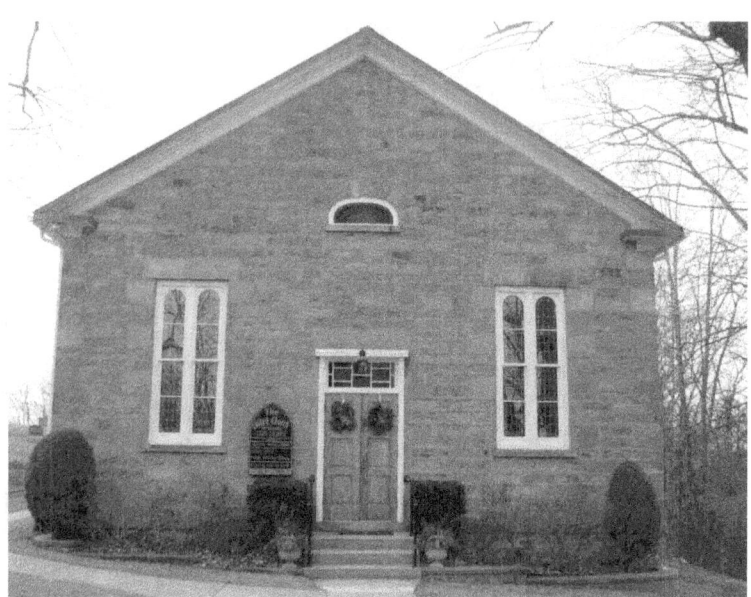

Glen Morris United Church – cobblestone

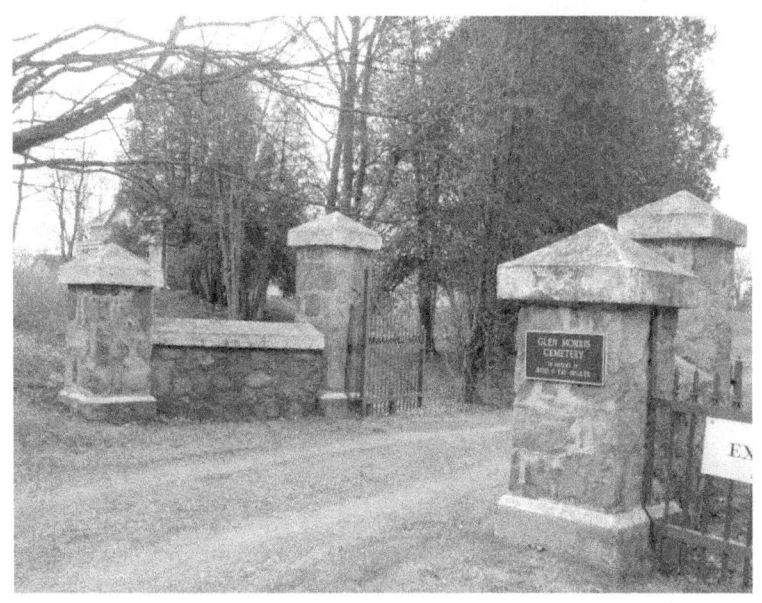

Glen Morris Cemetery – cobblestone gates

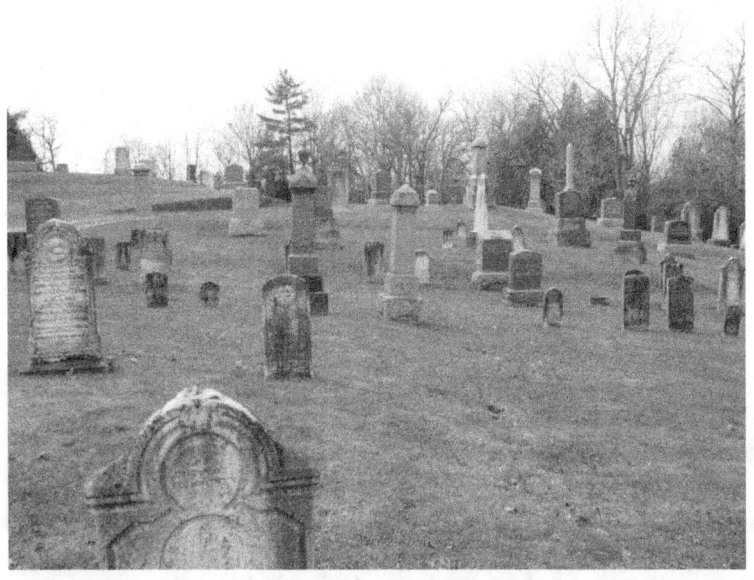

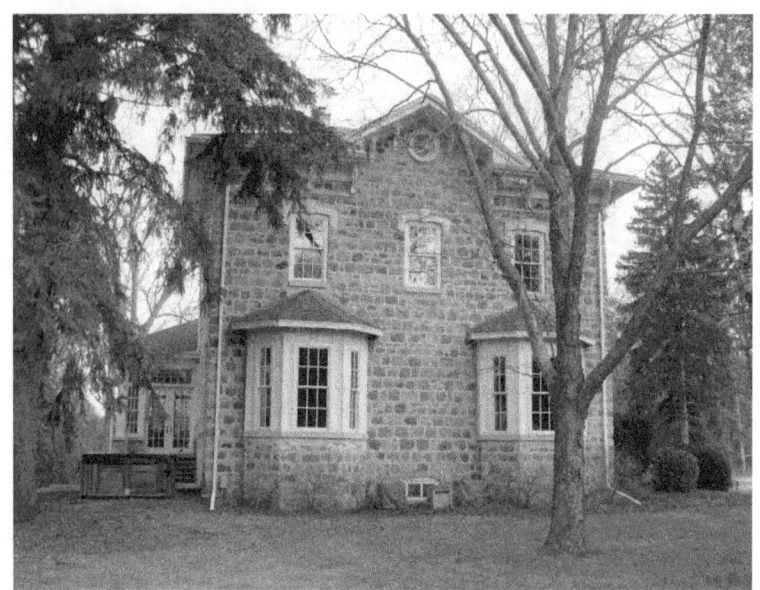

Cobblestone, bay windows, cornice brackets, small gable in attic with cornice return and round window

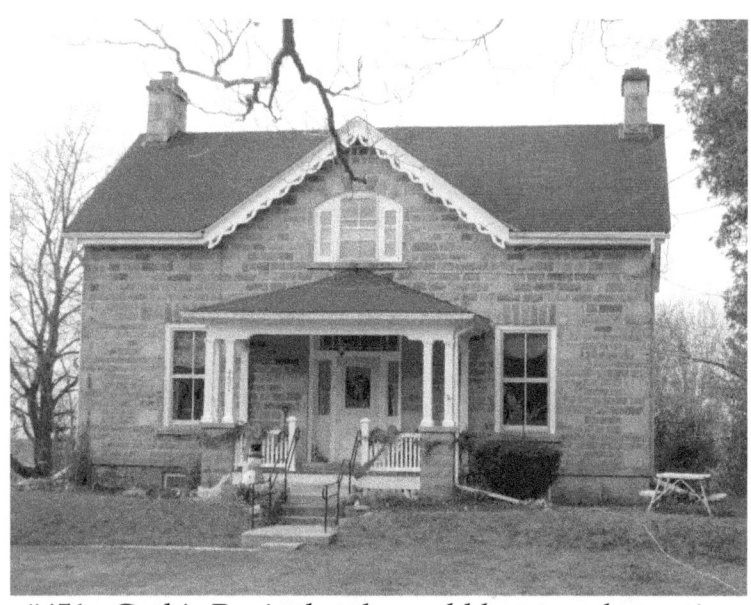

#451 - Gothic Revival style – cobblestone, decorative Vergeboard on gable

Architectural Terms

Belvedere: (from the Italian "beautiful view") an architectural feature on a roof, in a garden or on a terrace that gives a beautiful view. Example: Grand River Street North	
Brackets: a decorative or weight-bearing structural element which forms a right angle with one side against a wall and the other under a projecting surface such as an eave or roof. Example: 77 William Street	
Buttress: a masonry structure built against or projecting from a wall which serves to support or reinforce the wall. In Canadian architecture, they are sometimes used for decoration. Example: Sacred Heart Church, 17 Washington Street	
Cobblestone architecture: Refers to the use of cobblestones embedded in mortar as a method for erecting walls on houses and commercial buildings. Example: Sacred Heart Church, 17 Washington Street	
Cornice: originally the wooden overhang of the roof. With the use of stone, brick, iron and steel, the cornice is any projecting shelf at the top of a ceiling or roof. They can be very decorative.	
Cornice Return: decorative element on the end of a gable. Example: 83 Willow Street	

Cupola: a small, dome-like structure on top of a building often used to provide a lookout or to admit light and air. Example: Wisteria Cottage, Grand River Street North	
Dentil Moulding: an even series of rectangles used as ornamental decoration in cornices. Example: Downtown storefront	
Dichromatic brickwork: the use of two colours of brick, tile or slate to decorate a façade. Example: Steeple on Sacred Heart Church, 17 Washington Street	
Dormer: (French for "sleep") a gable end window that pierces through the plane of a sloping roof surface to create usable space in the top floor or attic of a building by adding headroom. Example: 57 Main Street	
Finial: ornament added to the top of a gable, pinnacle, canopy or spire – a Gothic element. Example: 48 Jane Street	
Frontispiece: a portion of the façade of a building, usually a centred doorway that is slightly raised from the rest of the building, usually with extensive ornamentation. Frontispieces are usually Classical in design with white columned porches. Example: 46 West Street	

Gable: the triangular portion of a wall between the edges of a sloping roof. Example: 48 Banfield Street	
Hipped Roof: a roof where all sides slope downwards to the walls with no gables.	
Keystones and Voussoirs: a voussoir is a wedge-shaped element used in building an arch. A keystone is the central stone that locks all the stones into position, allowing the arch to bear weight. A keystone is often enlarged and embellished. Example: 30 West Street	
Lancet Window: a tall, narrow window with a pointed arch at its top. Example: Paris Baptist Church, 25 Broadway Street West	
Lunette: A semi-circular area formed by an arch. Lunettes can either be windows or decorated areas at the end of a barrel vault. The windows were popular in Neo-classical and Classic Revival architecture in the 18th and 19th centuries in Canada. Example: 17 Washington Street	
Mansard Roof: This style was popularized by Francois Mansart (1598-1666), an accomplished architect of the French Baroque period and especially fashionable during the Second French Empire (1852-1870). This roof is almost flat on the top section, with two slopes on each of its sides with the lower slope at a steeper angle than the upper and having dormer windows. Example: 87 Willow Street	

Palladian Window: a large window that is divided into three sections with the centre section larger than the two side sections and usually arched. Example: 111 Willow Street	
Pediment: a triangular section above the horizontal structure (entablature), typically supported by columns. The inside of the triangle is called the tympanum. Example: 32 West Street	
Quoin: masonry blocks at the corner of a wall, often a decorative feature, usually larger or of a different colour than the rest of the wall. Example: 30 West Street	
Turret: a small tower that projects from the wall of a building. Example: 18 Banfield Street	
Rose Window: a circular window with ornamental tracery radiating from the centre. Example: 164 Grand River Street North.	
Vergeboards: also called bargeboards – hang from the projecting end of a roof and are often elaborately carved and ornamented. Example: Grand River Street North	

Paris' Building Styles

Chateau, 1880-1930 – This style is a grand adaptation of the sixteenth-century French chateaus of the Loire Valley. It has a steeply pitched gable roof, dormers, turrets, gables, conical towers, lunettes and iron cresting. Example: 106 Grand River Street North	
Georgian, before 1860 – This style began with the British King Georges in the 18th century. These buildings have balanced facades around a central door, medium-pitched gable roofs, and small paned windows. Example: 84 William Street	
Greek Revival: Pedimented gable; symmetrical shape; wide, plain frieze (horizontal band above doorway, windows and below the cornice); entry porch with columns; narrow windows around front door. Example: 52 Grand River Street South	
Regency Cottage, 1830-1860 – This style originated in England in 1815 and spread to Ontario later in the 19th century as British officers retired to Canada. It is a modest one-storey house with a low-pitched hip roof and has a symmetrical front façade. Example: 13 John Street	
Gothic Revival, 1830-1890 – These decorative buildings have sharply-pitched gables with highly detailed vergeboards, pointed-arch window openings, and dichromatic brickwork. It is a common style in Ontario. Example: 38 Jane Street	

Italianate, 1850-1900 – It has wide-bracketed eaves, belvederes, wrap-around verandahs. Example: 30 West Street	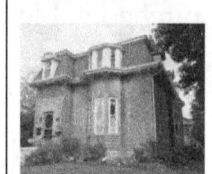
Second Empire, 1860-1880 – The mansard roof is the most noteworthy feature of this style and is evidence of the French origins. Projecting central towers and one or two-storey bays can also be present. Example: 87 Willow Street	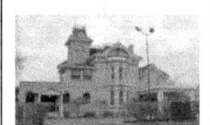
Queen Anne, 1885-1900 – This style is distinguished by an irregular outline featuring a combination of an offset tower, broad gables, projecting two-storey bays, verandahs, multi-sloped roofs, and tall, decorative chimneys. A mixture of brick and wood is common. Windows often have one large single-paned bottom sash and small panes in the upper sash. Example: 184 Grand River Street North	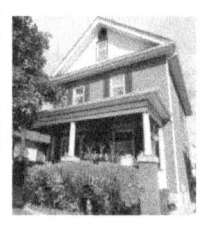
Edwardian, 1900-1930 – This style bridges the ornate and elaborate styles of the Victorian era and the simplified styles of the 20th century. Balanced facades, simple roof lines, dormer windows, large front porches, and smooth brick surfaces are its characteristics. Example: Willow Street	

www.ingramcontent.com/pod-product-compliance
Lightning Source LLC
Chambersburg PA
CBHW071800170526
45167CB00003B/1102